Olga Haub

D1505605

WITHIN A DARK WOOD

WITHIN A DARK WOOD

The Personal Story of a Rape Victim

by

Jennifer Barr

Doubleday & Company, Inc.
Garden City, New York
1979

ISBN: 0-385-15228-0
Library of Congress Catalog Card Number 79-6976
Copyright © 1979 by Jennifer Barr
All Rights Reserved
Printed in the United States of America
First Edition

This book is . . .

    . . . for those who seek awareness, that they may know what rape is;

    . . . for those who are concerned, that they may comprehend the chaos of a life shattered by rape;

    . . . for the parents, husbands, children, and friends of victims, who must endure their own pain while struggling to support the victim. This book is for them, that they may understand the vacant stares, the pounding fists, the angry screams, the quiet weeping in the night;

    . . . for other victims, that they might find comfort from a sister victim;

    . . . for future victims, that their struggles may be made easier by an aware and understanding society.

THIS book is a personal story. It is not a textbook on rape nor meant to be a guide on how victims react. My account of the journey of my mind reflects feelings shared by many victims, but each victim and each rape is unique. This is one victim's story.

This book began in my journal when I could not voice my thoughts openly. The notebooks I filled after the rape grew into this book as I detailed the episodes of that year. Journal entries left in their original form are included throughout this book.

Many people by chance or choice were a part of this story. For the sake of simplicity, many of the characters are composites of the actual people involved. For the sake of their privacy, I have changed names and have altered descriptions, backgrounds, or personalities when it did not affect the purpose of this book. I have depicted people as I saw them. If there are distortions, they are distortions that were in my mind at the time.

I could not have endured this experience without support from people who cared for me and believed in me. I am especially grateful to my husband who stayed by my side when I had nothing to give in return; to my friends who listened and waited patiently for me to smile again; to the Rape Crisis Center that supported me when I could not stand alone; to my counselor and my pastor who both helped me understand and accept; and I am grateful for my children who innocently accepted and never asked for an explanation.

In the middle of the journey of our life I came to myself within a dark wood where the straight way was lost.

Dante, *The Divine Comedy*

WITHIN A DARK WOOD

CHAPTER I

NIGEL was still in the midst of his temper tantrum when we arrived at Rosemary's house at nine-thirty on the morning of October 15. I smiled at my stubborn son in spite of his screams, as I looked forward to a few hours to myself on this beautiful autumn day. I would be leaving Nigel's demands and little Colin's needs with Rosemary for two unencumbered, undistracted hours. It seemed as if it had been a lifetime since I had enjoyed such freedom to wander as I wished.

With my baby in my arms and my two-year-old tempest attached to my leg, I maneuvered to the house.

"Hi, Rosemary. I'm here," I called from the door.

"I can tell!" She laughed. "I'm in the living room. Come on in."

I left Nigel banging at the door and laughed back. "What are *you* laughing at? *You're* the one who's going to have him all morning!"

Rosemary was sitting on the couch nursing her six-month-old baby, who had been born the day before my Colin. She tilted her head and pushed back her long dark hair, displaying clear blue eyes that precisely matched those of her offspring. "Want to fix yourself some coffee and sit down a minute?"

"Thanks, I will . . . as long as it's not docked from my two hours."

I brought my coffee into the living room and sat on the floor beside Colin. "Hey, babe, want one more feeding while I'm sitting here?" I didn't wait for any response as I tucked him into my lap to nurse while we talked.

We chatted about the elementary math course we were taking and laughed about how apprehensive we had been about enrolling. Rosemary and I had become friends when our recent pregnancies drew us together. Though I was not accustomed to close friendships and had been careful not to entwine our lives too deeply, the math class we enrolled in together insured that we saw each other at least once a week. By fall I felt comfortable enough with her to suggest the baby-sitting exchange. I did not realize that on that first day of baby-sitting our lives would be entwined more tenaciously than rabbits huddled against an arctic wind.

Rosemary and all the kids were in the doorway, waving as I drove away. Nigel, an independent critter, never seemed bothered by my leaving, but I had never left little Colin before. I hoped the morning would go smoothly for them all.

By the time I reached the highway and turned north, I was filled with a soaring feeling of freedom. No kids demanding my attention. Such quiet. It didn't matter where I went—it was the freedom, the idleness of my mind that I craved. Just being alone was such a luxury. I had planned to play tennis with Kathy that morning, but she had canceled when one of her girls had gotten sick. It would have been a perfect day for tennis. I had headed the car toward the library, but the library began to lose its appeal—the day was too beautiful to be inside. It was a day designed for the world to enjoy, to be in the midst of.

I circled back to the house to get my cameras. I hadn't been able to do much nature photography since becoming a mother, but I was inspired by the photographs Jon had taken on his hike in the Cascades that summer. I dreamed a moment about the old days when we toted our backpacks and cameras and drank from the streams together. There was a lake nearby with a path encircling it where we had taken family walks before. It wasn't the Cascades wilderness, but it would be a perfect area for photographing the foliage and fall fungi.

At the undeveloped end of the lake there had been an old dirt road down to the lakeshore. But housing construction had begun and that road was paved, ending abruptly in a cul-de-sac—signs of further human invasion into the quiet spots of the earth. I returned to the regular parking lot where there were paved paths and picnic tables. It just meant I had to walk farther to get to the woodlands.

There were two other cars in the parking lot, but no one was in sight. In spite of the beautiful weather, I had the lake almost to myself. I would have felt more comfortable to see a few more people there, but I laughed at the worry that passed through my head. "This isn't Central Park, after all!"

As I followed the narrow path that led away from the parking area, I could forget that there was a world beyond these woods. The world of the woods made no demands, produced only pleasant thoughts of beauty and stability and timelessness. Unmoving century-old trees beside ever-changing water gave a perspective of continuity and of acceptance. Nature following patterns with no struggle against inherent growth or change or death; no struggle for control of other creations beyond the struggle for self-survival. A tree demands nothing as it searches for its own nourishment, yet in its independence and self-determination it provides rest, shelter, nutrition, and beauty by its existence. No demands, no expectations of help from others, no desire to control or destroy. Each element of nature exists, merely exists, and in that existence creates a unique beauty, a peace. Alone in the woods even a human can feel that acceptance of existence, without questions, doubts, struggles. Perfect tranquillity and peace can be found where even man is but another element of the woods.

Some ducks were sitting on a log in the lake. I stood and watched them before I took out the camera and changed to the telephoto lens. Each duck was evenly spaced along the log, seemingly oblivious to each other yet gathered together by some unspoken need. When I clicked the shutter only one duck raised its head in momentary alarm. I moved to another angle to get the lineup of ducks silhouetted by the sunshine in back. The angle that I wanted was blocked by heavy bushes along the lakeshore, but I was satisfied with my less dramatic shot.

As I stood up from my crouched position I looked up at the trees directly above me. It was an artist's pallet of colors converging in contrast to the azure sky. I switched to the camera with color film in an attempt to capture perfect autumn in one print.

I had planned to walk all the way around the lake, but as I approached the upper end I found the path was washed out in a large marshy area. There had been wet spots all along the trail, but this was more than a puddle or a stream crossing, with deep mud extending into the woods. As I looked for a route around the mud, I noticed a man standing on the bridge not far ahead. He was leaning on the railing, looking at the lake with his back towards me. I checked the time and decided if I turned back at that point, I could still stop at the library. I felt rejuvenated and ready to take my tranquilized mind back to the busy life.

I paused to work on one more photo but couldn't capture the feeling I wanted. When I returned to the path, I noticed that the man on the bridge was no longer in sight. I was glad we did not meet deep in the woods. I didn't want to have to acknowledge another human being yet.

Since the shutter was still cocked, instead of returning the cameras to the camera bag I looked for something to use that shot on. As I came up the path where it leaves the water's edge and rounds a bend, a middle-aged man approached, carrying his jacket over his shoulder. I nodded a "Good morning," but he didn't return the nod. He passed by briskly.

Suddenly my head was jerked back with the force of a collision. The autumn colors swirled around me. The sky was endless blue above. An arm wrapped my neck like an iron vise. Terror stopped time. I screamed instinctively, un-knowingly.

The scream was outside me. I heard it but did not feel it. Inside, I was the blue sky. I was part of it. It was all I was conscious of. It was my existence. It was death. It was an escape from the screaming.

A low tense voice made me aware that life still existed.

"Stop screaming!" The voice was tenser as he repeated his order. His grip tightened around my neck and mouth. My mind had no power over the scream. My mind had no power. Thoughts pounded through my head as I tried to understand what was happening. Was this a joke? Was this someone I knew being cruel? It couldn't be real. What did he want?

As I struggled to escape his grip a knife flashed at my throat. It wasn't a joke.

"Shut up or I'll kill you!" My scream faded. My struggle froze. My mind gasped for reason, order, sanity. We had lost our cameras in a burglary once—the cameras must be what he wanted. I had a lot of money hanging around my neck—hanging crisscross around my neck, limiting my motions like a ball and chain. But he didn't have to kill me to get them. He didn't have to pull me backwards into the woods.

My glasses fell off and I automatically tried to retrieve them. "Wait—I can't lose my glasses." He held me while I stooped to pick them up.

The knife was at my ribs; his arm still gripped my neck as he pulled me towards an old overgrown roadbed. The hand left my neck and slid inside my pants to grasp my bottom.

"Nice ass," he said, as if it were a compliment. My feet

stopped moving and I began to tremble. Reality was beginning to sink in. It wasn't the cameras he was after.

"What's the matter?" The voice was still low.

"I'm scared."

"Just do what I say and I won't hurt you."

"I just had a baby." It was my attempt to tell him I was
human, to tell him I was needed. It wasn't a calculated
statement, it was a reflexive defense.

"I'm not going to rape you. I'm not going to hurt you if
you don't scream or do anything stupid."

Rape! I felt my insides collapse at the sound of the
word. I had thought no further than that I was in life-threat-
ening danger. *Rape! God, that doesn't happen. What does
he want? What is he going to do to me?* My mind was fran-
tic to know the future, to consider my options. I was aware
survival was my ultimate goal. *Whatever he wants as long
as he doesn't use the knife.* I grasped for the defense instructions that every woman hears and no woman thinks she'll
ever need.

I quickly evaluated my chances of escape. Could I
break away and run? The weeds were high; my cameras
were heavy and awkward. I didn't know what I was dealing
with; I couldn't see him to know his size or strength. I didn't
know if I could outrun him, and if I tripped he'd be on top
of me with the knife.

I tried to think of what I could say to make him realize
I was human, to make him decide he didn't want to hurt me.
He had shown some human instinct in letting me get my
glasses. His tone and words seemed to want to reassure me,
to comfort me. Pleading seemed my most hopeful tactic.

"Please let me go. I have to get home." It was feeble and didn't illicit any response.

He didn't seem certain of where he wanted to go but finally motioned to a thicket. "Over there." The bushes and weeds were three to four feet high and our feet sank in the thick layer of honeysuckle that covered everything. Beyond the bushes the no-longer green weeds still stood waiting for the last seed pods to fall. We were out of sight of the lake, but the path was still visible from where we stood.

His hand pushed down past my stomach inside my pants.

"Feels like you're ready."

God, what did he want? He said he wasn't going to rape me. Ready? Ready for what? Why did he say that? How could I feel ready for anything? What was he talking about? Mister, whatever you want just get it over with and let me go!

He told me to put down the cameras. Maybe that was still all he wanted. Maybe he would just grab them and leave. I put them down.

"Take off your clothes. Not your shoes." He was standing behind me at the entrance to the thicket. There was no choice. Slowly I took off my clothes except my bra. As he unhooked my bra, I pleaded, "I'm nursing a baby. My baby . . ." My baby mattered, my baby was still real.

With one hand he reached around me and clutched each breast.

He told me to kneel, then stepped in front of me. His pants were off and he thrust his penis at my mouth.

"Suck it!"

My teeth were cemented together with all the power in

my body. I glanced around me. It was the first time the man was visible. Above me I could see only a large belly. To my left I saw the knife in a clenched fist.

"Suck it!" He held my head as he pushed his penis past my lips. My teeth parted slightly. I held it there, tempted to bite but the risk was too great.

"Suck it harder!" and he pushed it to the back of my mouth. He was tense at my resistance and I felt the knife brush my hair as he used both hands to hold my head. I gagged till he let go of my head and I was able to back off a bit. He unbuttoned his shirt while his penis was in my mouth. At least he seemed clean.

He stepped back and told me to lie down. I hesitated. He took off his shirt and threw it down for me to lie on.

"There. Put your face on it." He still had his undershirt, shoes, hat, and sunglasses on. He pulled his undershirt up to his armpits.

I lay down slightly on my side so that I could see him. He stepped behind me and knelt out of my sight.

"I have a baby," I repeated. I wanted to talk to him, to make him aware of what he was doing, but my mind was stuck on the one plea. How long would it be before I saw my baby again? Who would take care of him? What was he doing now? I needed to get back to him. I'd never left him before. It was my last effort to keep my identity. I ceased any attempt to feel like me, to feel human, to feel. In order to endure, I had to abandon the idea that I was a person. My mind was not prepared to deal with what was happening. It was not reality, but if it wasn't real, neither was the sky, nor time, nor me.

"Shut up" was his sympathy. I felt his hands, then his fingers, then his face in my bottom.

"Does that feel good?"

He expected an answer and I responded noncommittally and without imagination. "It's hard to say under the circumstances."

"Roll over." He pulled my leg over and watched my body as I turned. "When was your last good fuck?"

What does he want me to say? I've never had it so good? It's been so long? I didn't respond.

He mounted my chest and lifted my head to his penis, ordering me to suck it again. I didn't struggle. He still held the knife and I was afraid that in his tenseness I would be cut if I didn't move the way he expected me to.

I tried to think of something to say, something to reach whatever humane feelings he had. *Do you come here often? Are you married?* What can one say to a stranger?

As he backed off my chest, he grasped my breasts and sucked at the right nipple. He didn't suck long; perhaps the unexpected taste of my baby's milk made me too real. He knelt between my legs and pushed my knees to my chest. My attempts to maintain human emotions and thoughts completely ceased. I was a creature striving for survival, my mind frozen in the uncertainty of what would come next, struggling only with the moment.

"Spread your cunts." I didn't understand. When I hesitated, he leaned forward and pushed my thighs apart. He examined my exposed genitals with the intensity of a grooming baboon.

He wanted me to masturbate myself. I complied passively.

"Not that finger!" and he pushed my second finger into my vagina. He tensely masturbated himself and told me to massage his scrotum. Still not satisfied with his progress, he leaned forward to rub his penis against my clitoris. I lay very still, hoping to have it over with as soon as possible. Suddenly his penis slid back to my vagina and I squirmed with the pain of the pressure against my tense muscles.

"Hold still! I'm not going to rape you!" he snarled, but he pulled back. He climbed back onto my chest and masturbated anxiously, his face dripping sweat.

It would have to be over soon, but the time wasn't moving. And what then? I looked at the unmoving weeds near my face, and the sky beyond. It was all a movie I was forced to watch. The trees were all stoically watching between the sky and the weeds. But in a movie the wind and clouds would have erased the blue sky. Why wouldn't he kill me? He had the power, the violence, the hatred, the weapon to make him capable of it. How else could this ordeal end? He would have to kill me to get away with this. I saw my gory naked body being found by some Sunday-afternoon hiker, or lovers looking for a nest. I thought of the kids and of Jon. Life would go on. They would survive. Nigel and Colin would be cared for and loved, but what effect would the knowledge of this event have on them even if they didn't remember their mama.

In the midst of my defeat an awareness of a power I still held came to me. With all his power he could not control my mind. If I survived I could identify him. I began to concentrate, carefully, calculatingly, on the details of his anatomy. I took quick glances at his face, unable to stare eye to eye. After each glance I reviewed what I had seen as

I would have if I were memorizing Latin conjugations. I searched his face, his neck, his chest, his stomach, his arms for any identifying or distinctive marks. It occupied my mind and gave me a feeling of control, however slight.

As he was coming to a climax, I knew what he wanted. He held my head but my face was turned away and my mouth tightly closed. As he ejaculated he couldn't force his penis past my teeth, so he pushed it against my nose. A lot of semen went up my nose and I fought the gagging which would have opened my mouth. When he was spent, he spread the semen over my face and into my hair.

I lay numb and motionless as he backed off me. My fate was still in his hands. Defeated in the hands of the enemy, I didn't want him to prove his power further. I had ceased being human early in the game and had no self to protect anymore. I did not fear death, I was past fear, but my life hinged on his total victory.

I did not move until he ordered me to sit up. He was searching the ground under me. His tenseness was again apparent.

"Help me find it!" he demanded.

I assumed it was the knife he was so anxious to find. How long would he stay to search? I just wanted him to leave. I looked around, using the time to check for more details. I could see his whole body. I saw a brassy object in the weeds near me. Beyond it was his broad white back. I contemplated my reach. I contemplated the risk. Could I use it if I had the knife in my hand? Could I live with myself afterwards if I plunged that blade into soft human flesh? And if I failed in the attempt . . . ? He saw it too before I reached a decision. He picked it up and held it as he dressed.

As I watched him dress, I observed every item of clothing. He picked up my blouse and pants and turned to leave.

"I'll leave them where you can find them. Don't scream or try to follow me or I'll come back." As if I ever wanted to see him again! I watched as he dropped my clothes near the lake and disappeared behind the shrubbery.

I put on my underwear and methodically put the cameras in the camera bag. The camera that had been lying beside me still had its shutter cocked. If I had elbowed the shutter release, I might have gotten a picture of him. But I didn't need a photograph to remember that face. He'd never get away with this. I could identify him by his smell alone if he ever came near me again. Let him walk off now in conquest, but he'd never get away with this.

I finished dressing on the path where I found my clothes and followed the path to my car. I walked in complete control—the complete control of a robot. The trees could have been gray concrete walls, the woodland sounds could have been sirens for all my awareness of them. I drove directly home and called the police.

"Hello. I was just sexually assaulted." I was emotionless.

"What is your name? . . . Your address? . . . Your phone number? . . . When did it happen? . . . Where? . . . Can you give me a description? . . . Were you raped? . . . Are you at home now or do you want to meet the officer at the hospital?"

"No, I wasn't raped. . . . No, I wasn't injured. I'll be waiting at my home. I'm not going anywhere."

"An officer will be right over."

As methodically as I had dialed the police I dialed Jon.

"I'm sorry Mr. Barr is not in his office right now. Can I take a message?"

"Please find him and tell him to call home as soon as possible." I wanted to be sure he would get the message without creating alarm. I hadn't thought what I would say to him, I just wanted him home.

I sat on the kitchen stool in a daze till the phone rang a few minutes later.

"Jon, can you come home." It wasn't a question.

"What's the matter?" *Why? Does something have to be the matter? Just come home.*

"I need you. . . . I . . . I was assaulted."

I didn't move from the kitchen stool. I didn't think. I picked at the burrs on my pants as the world waited. I should have known not to wear polyester slacks in the woods.

CHAPTER II

I HEARD Jon's car swerve into the driveway, and without moving my mind or body, I watched him enter the house.

Though the speed of his car had shown his anxiety, he seemed only concerned as he approached me. I had not thought about how he would react or what he might be thinking. I was only aware of my need for his presence. I needed him physically near me, but my mind was still frozen, still surviving each moment by animal instinct.

"Are you O.K.?" I heard him ask. I pulled away as he tried to hug me to him. I was dirty and not ready to give or receive.

"I'm O.K." I was staring at my hands again.

"Were you raped?" He stood beside me, still holding my shoulders, hoping I would respond.

"No." My voice was flat and muted. I felt no need to tell him what happened. He had to understand without the words, without the details.

"Did you call the police?"

"Yes, they're coming."

Then there was silence. We waited together. He didn't push me to talk.

"Are the kids still with Rosemary?" he asked finally.

"Yes."

"Did you talk to her?"

"No." I hadn't thought to call her. It was ten minutes till I was due to pick up the kids. I had no knowledge of what would happen when the police arrived, how long it would be, what would happen afterwards. Neither the future nor past were real.

"I'd better call her." He didn't consult me. He didn't require a decision from me on how to handle the situation. Though he must have been confused by my composure and uncertain about my quietness, he automatically assumed the responsibility of caring for the necessities I was oblivious to.

"Rosemary? This is Jon. Can you keep the kids a while longer? . . . Jenn . . . had a bad morning. I'm not sure how long it will be. Are they O.K.? . . . Thanks a lot, we'll get them as soon as we can."

I had no thoughts about what Rosemary might think, no thoughts about the kids. I watched Jon and listened to his words but they were meaningless.

"Was it at the library?" He knew I'd mentioned going there. He asked without pressure.

"I went to the lake . . . to take pictures." I looked at

his eyes for the first time to see if he saw the irony in the freedom I had sought.

He reached down to kiss me, to kiss my semen-coated face. "Don't . . . no, don't . . . oh, wait, it's O.K. . . . You can kiss me here," and I pointed to a clean spot on my jaw that I thrust towards him. It was a gentle slow kiss. A kiss of acceptance of unknown reasons, a kiss of love without questions. I accepted his kiss.

Jon went to the window when a car approached. "It's the police, Jenn." No siren, no flashing lights. It didn't move the air inside.

I moved from the stool to the kitchen doorway while Jon opened the door. The officer stepped inside and glanced past Jon at me.

"My name is Burke. Sorry I took so long to get here." He took off his hat and ran his fingers through his thick blond hair, unsure of which of us he was talking to.

"I went to the lake first. . . . I had planned on patrolling that area this morning. This isn't the first incident there. I was going out there as soon as I got out of court. I got your call as soon as I got into my car. I would have been there this morning. . . ." His words were quiet but did not hide an intensity of feeling that I didn't expect from a policeman.

He followed Jon into the living room and stood waiting as I moved to the closest chair.

"Do you want your husband to stay?" He spoke directly to me. He gave no hint of his preference. It was my choice. I looked at Jon but he was open to my decision too.

"Do you really want to hear it, Jon?" I didn't want him to listen but I wanted him to stay.

"Whichever is easier for you, Mrs. Barr," Burke interjected, then turned to Jon, "Why don't you stay for a while anyway?"

For once I wasn't bothered that decisions were being made for me. I had gotten myself home and called for help. I had done what had to be done and had no direction left. Jon sat down in the closest chair to me.

"Can you tell me what happened?" Burke stood with his hat held under one arm and his pencil and clipboard ready.

I didn't move, I didn't look up as I tried to find words to answer his question. The words came slowly through my teeth. "He made me suck him." My jaw tensed. Jon heard it. My eyes fastened on a spot on the rug.

Burke sat down on the couch across the room without asking an explanation of my statement.

"Can you describe the area where it happened? What time did it happen?" He asked his questions slowly and with concern. "Can you describe the man? Did he threaten you? Did he have a weapon? Did you struggle? Did you scream? Did you see how he left the area?" He didn't ask for any-more sexual details.

I cranked out the answers, moving only my lips. My descriptions were detailed. I had no problem with recall. Jon served as an interpreter when he felt I didn't understand the question or Burke didn't understand my answer. His comments broke my tension enough that I could look up and know he was still there.

We went over the descriptions a number of times until he was satisfied he had gotten as many details as he could from me. He pulled out a drawing he had with his papers and asked if it looked like the same man. There was resemblance. "That was done by a sixteen-year-old girl two weeks ago who was grabbed at the lake and escaped. I'm sure it was the same guy. That's who I was going to the lake to look for this morning . . . and I would have found him. We'll get him yet. Sorry we didn't get him soon enough."

"Well, is there a chance . . . ?" My question seemed awkward. "I mean, is there danger . . . ? Could he find out about me if he's out on bail or something?"

"You've been watching too much late-night TV. Don't worry about it." I resented the assumption. It was a real question, a real fear, but I felt foolish to have asked.

"Do you have a baby?" He saw the portacrib in the dining room as he rose.

"Six months old," Jon said.

He winced and turned to Jon, taking a deep breath. "I know how I'd feel if I were in your situation, but take it easy. Don't try to do anything heroic. That's our job. She needs your support now more than anything else. Now, Mrs. Barr, one of the detectives might want to talk to you more later. They are pretty busy right now, but they may need some more information and might call you about it. Do you want me to take you over to the hospital?"

I wasn't injured, I just needed rest. I was prepared for the ordeal to be over when he left. I didn't want to prolong it. "I'm O.K."

"If you think of anything more, call me." He gave me his card and left.

I looked around the room as I leaned against the kitchen door. The drapes were still closed from morning. The house was unusually clean. I was glad I didn't have the added humility of dirty clothes lying on the floor or the breakfast dishes still on the table. It had been one of my organized mornings.

"What now?" Time was still meaningless. I felt the pull of transition—what had to be done was finished. I needed to move back into my world again.

"I don't know, Jenn. . . ." We looked at each other for a lost moment. "I guess I'll go pick up the kids, O.K.?"

"Yeah. Poor Rosemary got more than she bargained for. I guess I'll take a shower."

Jon followed me to the bedroom to be sure it was all right to leave me. "Yeah. I just need to clean up and then lie down a bit. I'm O.K."

I stood in the shower and let the water stream over my face and body. With all my scrubbing, nothing felt cleaner. I didn't want to get out. It was my only hope of cleansing myself. The smell wouldn't go away. I stood motionless as the water formed a membrane around me. It pulsed out all sounds. It blurred all sight. My total awareness was the water. I couldn't go back to that other world.

Jon came into the bathroom to check on me and I became aware of the children's voices. I delivered myself back to the world to greet them. They had been fed and were ready for naps. Rosemary had even nursed Colin after Jon called her. They made no requirements of me, so I let Jon put them to bed.

I lay down on the bed to sleep but welcomed Jon when he entered and lay down beside me. It was good just to be close to him. I didn't want to talk about the morning. He had heard enough.

"Did Rosemary say how it went with the kids this

morning?" I lay very still, talking to the ceiling or to a flower on the wallpaper as I turned toward Jon.

"No. She said Colin was fussy at lunchtime. That's why she nursed him when she found out you wouldn't be there at noon."

"Did you say anything to her?"

"No. I figured it was for you to talk about. I'd better let you get some sleep while the kids are sleeping."

He got up to leave and hesitated. "Should I stay?"

"Kiss me." He sat down beside me and gave a gentle kiss. My arms locked around him until he lay down on me. I wanted him to crush me. I wanted him to open his ribs and let me crawl in. I closed my eyes as the weight on top of me made my body disappear between him and the mattress. When he thought I was asleep, he got up to leave. My eyes opened and I watched but let him go.

The shade had been pulled so the room was dimly lit. I didn't move. I couldn't move. I waited for sleep but my eyes followed the swerving blue onions on the wallpaper. I didn't think about the assault. I thought about how the patrolman had reacted, what he had said, what would he do next. The thoughts came slowly and repetitiously. I didn't sleep. I heard the kids awaken one by one but still I did not move. Finally I heard Jon in the kitchen beginning supper and I gave up on sleep. I went into the kitchen to help.

"Just sit down, Jenn. I can handle it."

I had no doubts about his cooking; he often cooked when I asked for help. I was grateful but restless.

"Colin probably wants to nurse." I took him into the dining room and sat down to nurse him. He latched on to my left breast anxiously, unaware of any doubts I had about the cleanness of my body. I limited my concerns to my right breast, the one that had been sucked, and relaxed in my usefulness to admire my son. He was so beautiful. It was such a joy to nurse him, to see such contentment. Sweat beads formed on his nose at the intensity of his nursing. His big eyes glanced up occasionally with a twinkle, then his eyelids drooped as he resumed his concentration. I smoothed his wisps of hair back from his forehead. His skin was so soft. His babyhood was slipping away so quickly. I'd been able to spend much more time with Nigel, but now my attention was divided. With a two-year-old demanding more than his share of attention, I had little time or energy to just enjoy my baby. I was glad I was still nursing; it guaranteed private moments between Colin and me.

At supper Jon remarked about how well I was taking the incident.

"What would you expect? Hysteria? There's no reason for hysteria now. It's over. It was just a stupid thing. TV always has to make a big deal of everything, gives such a distorted picture. It's just like the way it portrays women in childbirth—writhing and screaming. It just makes a good story. I'm not going to let some jerk ruin my life. It's over and done with. I'm O.K."

"Are you going to class tonight?"

"Yeah. She counts attendance in grading. I'm not going to blow an A on this rinky-dink course. Rosemary is driving tonight anyway."

I saw no reason not to go. Class would fill a few more hours; it would be a distraction to help me forget.

After supper I sat down in the rocker in Colin's dark room to nurse him. Again I nursed him on my left side. He was squirmy and didn't settle down quickly. He alternated between the pacifier and the nipple until he began to droop. Finally his head dropped back with his little mouth still forming a circle. He hardly stirred as I moved him to his crib.

Rosemary had already arrived when I finished. I gathered my books and kissed Nigel good night.

The front seat of her VW was filled by the infant seat, so she got out to let me into the back seat.

"Are you O.K.?"

"Yes."

"Were you assaulted?" I looked at her, unprepared for the question.

"Yes." And I climbed into the car.

"Did you go to the library?"

"No, I went to the lake." I talked to the back of her head. It was a quiet drive.

In class I sat next to the window and stared into the blackness beyond. Though I wasn't listening, I followed mechanically the evening's lesson. I spoke to no one until I was back in the car with Rosemary. We were halfway home before the silence was broken.

"I can't believe this happened," Rosemary said, uncomfortable with the silence. She was in her own agony.

"I'm just glad I'm not sixteen. I can't imagine . . . Here I am a married woman. It's not like something I didn't know happened but I feel so dumb. . . . I don't know how to even say it. . . . I mean, I'm not a kid. It's just so dumb. . . ." I tightened my arms around my chest and my side hurt. "I can still feel the knife in my ribs even . . ."

"I don't understand. Were you raped?"

"No, not exactly. Rape isn't the only torture method." It would have been simpler to just say I was raped, but I couldn't. I felt that I should explain.

"I think I understand." She didn't ask for more details. I didn't volunteer any.

When I got home, I went directly to the bedroom to go to bed. Jon followed.

"Jenn, when I was picking up this evening I noticed blood on your shirt . . ."

"Blood?" I was in the midst of changing into my nightie.

"Yeah. Look at your side." When I looked in the mirror, I realized why I still felt like I had the knife in my ribs. A series of crisp cuts, caked with dark, dried blood, lined my side.

"God, I'm really alert here. My ribs probably could have been broken and I wouldn't know it!"

It was a quiet, still night as I lay sleepless, thoughtless, bodiless into the darkness. *Tomorrow I would be fine. It was just a bad experience that ruined a beautiful day.*

Jon stayed home to let me sleep late the next morning. The house was quiet when I awoke. I rolled my face back into my pillow and groaned in the realization that I needed to nurse Colin. My right breast was swollen and leaking in fullness. My body felt unusually heavy in getting out of bed. Though I had slept for nine hours, I still felt very tired.

Reluctantly I let Colin nurse at the full right breast. I tried not to think about it. He didn't seem to notice any difference and nursed contentedly.

Jon and I tried to treat it like a normal morning; we didn't talk about the incident or anything related to it. Jon was very attentive to my needs, urging me to try to rest while he took care of the kids. After he put them down for naps, he asked if I'd mind his going in to pick up some papers at work.

"Sure. I'm O.K. I'll nap while the kids are sleeping." I lay down before he left and he followed me. I reached out to him and we cuddled and we made love with an intensity I didn't often feel. I was left with the desire for more. For the next few weeks I wanted him to constantly hold me and caress me. I needed to be told I was still desirable. I needed the total affection of someone. It was an escape to a prettier world where I was beautiful, loved, and protected.

I lay staring at the walls, waiting to sleep but sleep wouldn't come. My thoughts drummed out the minutes. *He could have killed me. He could have slit my throat. He could have cut me into pieces as I just lay there. Death could have come in an instant. How could I take care of my babes if I couldn't even take care of myself?* I felt the initial terror over and over. My neck and shoulders would stiffen as an unseen arm jolted me into eternity. *How easily he could have killed me.* Death and terror were still very real.

The phone intruded the stillness.

"Mrs. Barr? This is Detective Jameson from the police department. How are you today?"

"Uh . . . O.K."

"I need to ask you some more questions and I wonder if you could come down to the police station." His voice was soft and patient.

"My husband isn't home. I need to arrange it . . . a baby-sitter. I don't know."

"I'll be on duty till eleven tonight, so anytime this evening would be fine. Do you know when your husband will get home?"

"No . . . maybe about five. He should be home by then."

"Can we arrange it for six?"

"Well, supper . . . maybe earlier. I don't know. Yes, I guess five-thirty would be reasonable. How long will it take?"

"Maybe half hour or forty-five minutes. It depends on how long it takes to tell it, but it shouldn't take long."

"O.K."

"Do you know where the police station is? . . . Good, when you get here just ask for me at the front desk. I'll be looking for you then."

I lay back down wondering what information they wanted, why I had to go into the police station to answer questions. I was curious about the procedure; I had never been in a station before.

When we got to the station, Detective Jameson came out to escort me back to his department. He was younger than he sounded on the phone and not very tall. He asked Jon to wait in the lobby while we talked. The station seemed to be a maze of halls and large rooms, which we went through to a small interviewing room only large enough for two straight chairs and a small table.

"Please sit down," he said as he closed the door behind him.

"I'm sorry to have to bring you in, but I need to go over the story with you again." Again? He didn't just have a couple questions that needed clarification. He wanted more than that.

"I know this is very difficult for you, but we need to start at the beginning. . . ." He turned on a small tape recorder, stating the date and identifying himself.

"Can you state your name and address please . . . O.K. Now can we begin with when you left the house yesterday morning?"

The words stuck in my throat as I described why I went to the lake. Jameson had large, soft, sad eyes that watched me closely. He seemed very sympathetic and understanding. He laughed at my attempts at humor to break the tension. He gently led me from one statement to another. When I couldn't answer, he rephrased the question. When I didn't answer, he returned to the areas I was more comfortable discussing.

"I need to know exactly what he did to you, exactly what he said. As well as you can remember, Mrs. Barr. We need to try to learn his modus operandi, to be able to associate him with other crimes. Anything he said or did, his language, his words can give us a clue."

I couldn't repeat the words he used, many of them I heard for the first time and learned the meaning of during the assault. I was not used to discussing sexual details with anyone and found my vocabulary limited. I used terms that are associated with lovemaking—"fondled," "kissed"—and was embarrassed and repulsed by their use. I also felt embarrassed to be a wife and mother and not be able to explain what happened.

My description centered on the hatred and violence rather than the sexual acts. "I tried to talk to him. . . . I was so afraid he'd panic or lose his temper. . . . He had the knife, at my throat. . . ." His methods weren't important except that they successfully defeated me. He had no right to intrude on my life and toss my existence around. The sexual acts I was able to describe were to help in identifying him, to link him with other crimes. My mind was still too confused to give a step-by-step account of the event.

It took longer than he had estimated to tape the story.

"Were you taken to the hospital?"

"No. I probably should have been. I wasn't thinking very well. I was so numb I wasn't even aware I'd been cut. I could have been hurt worse and not realized it then."

"You were cut?"

"Just little cuts. It's more of a bruise now."

"I'll find someone to photograph that later."

Photograph it! It's only a bruise. It's on my ribs, just below my bra. Nothing worth photographing! I felt embarrassed to have mentioned it. I realized I was sitting with my arm boldly propped on the back of the chair. *Good grief, what will he think of me sitting like that!* My hand quickly returned to my lap to clutch my purse strap.

Finally he turned off the tape recorder and went to get Jon and a cup of coffee for me. I had to concentrate to steady my hands to drink the coffee, but my parched mouth soaked in the moisture like desert sand. Jon sat beside me and held my hand, knowing I was too exhausted to talk.

Detective Jameson returned and ushered me into another office and introduced me to a detective who would help me put together a composite picture of the man. Jameson left as I went through the kit trying to choose the sample eyes, nose, mouth that most closely resembled my attacker. The selection seemed poor and none of the relaxed features could match the sweat-dripping hatred of his face.

Jameson returned and left the door open behind him. "How are you doing?" I was glad to see his gentle smile again.

"I don't know. It's hard to show a lopsided nose or crooked teeth with the selection here."

"I know what you mean. Some things are hard to show on a drawing. I think I've found a photographer for you now, if you'd like to follow me."

I followed him through the maze of rooms and halls again and was introduced to a young woman holding an Instamatic camera. Jameson gave her instructions about the type and number of shots he wanted. We used the ladies' room for a studio.

The room was small and she had to stand in a booth to get enough distance for a full body shot. The booth's door swung shut and we giggled in the efforts to prop it open. Finally she held it with her foot. I posed in my bra, feeling absurd. *Should I smile for my photo or hide my face?* "No, hold your head up. We need this shot to identify who the bruise belongs to." The flash did not fire the first time, nor the second. She went out to find a new cube. Again the camera didn't work. It had no film. I was beginning to giggle hysterically at the scenario. There was no place for me to hide from view when she opened the door to get help with the camera. Jon could have done this at home much easier.

I was glad when I was through with that and back in Jameson's care.

"Well, thank you for coming in tonight. I think we got all the information that we need, but if there is anything else you think of, don't hesitate to call. Every detail is important. Are you O.K. now? Try to get some rest tonight. I know this hasn't been easy for you, but I really appreciate your coming in. Here comes your husband. Now remember to call if you think of anything more."

It was dark when we left the police station. Jon put his arm around me as we walked. I shivered even after we were in the car.

"Should we stop for something to eat?"

"No."

"A doughnut and coffee?"

"I just want coffee but I can wait till we get home."

"It was pretty rough, huh?"

"Just exhausting. I'm really tired. Wish you could have taken the photo of my bruise. It was really ridiculous. So dumb. Such an ordeal with a simple Instamatic."

"They just took a picture of the bruise on your side?"

"Yeah . . . just."

"Were you talking to Jameson the whole time I was waiting?"

"Yeah. What time is it now?"

"After seven-thirty."

"Wonder if the kids got supper." I watched the headlights pass us and the dark shadows beyond. Just shapes and darkness and a spectrum of grays.

As I lay on the bed that evening, Jon came in.

"I have to call the pastor tonight about the service on Sunday. Should I say something to him?" While our church was without a minister, Jon was in charge of finding fill-ins for the services. One pastor was our standard substitute and Jon worked with him whenever he was available. He should know, I thought. It would be awkward for Jon if he didn't. A minister's function is to help deal with crises. Maybe he could put things into perspective, could explain the order of things. An authority on living who could talk to me, who could tell me.

"Yes. That would be all right, Jon."

Jon arranged for the pastor to come by to talk to me the next morning and waited for him to arrive before he went in to work.

"Do you want to tell me about it, Jennifer?" He seemed tense and didn't look at me when he asked.

"He just grabbed me and it won't go away. I feel it over and over."

"I imagine it was very frightening. You weren't hurt though, were you?"

"No."

"You were lucky. You can't ever tell what a criminal mind might decide to do. What is it that bothers you so?"

"I don't know. It's just the terror."

"Where did it happen?"

"At the lake."

"So there's no fear he'll come back? He doesn't know where you live, does he?"

"No."

He searched for the basis for my feelings. I wanted reassurance and he wanted me to tell him why.

"You know you have two babies that are dependent on you right now and you can't go to pieces over this. You are bound to feel frightened by it. It hasn't even been forty-eight hours since it happened. Of course, you're upset, but you have to just put it behind you. I really can't do anything for you; you are the one who has to face it and deal with it."

I felt ashamed that I'd asked him to come. I was being

melodramatic. He had more important things to do than talk to me. He was right, he couldn't help me. When he left, I felt sealed in my isolation. He didn't seem to realize how empty I was, that there was nothing there except fear.

I spent the rest of the day with Rosemary. It was another pretty day, but I sat in her living room in the corner farthest from the windows. It was a quiet visit. I needed company, I needed someone to distract me, I needed someone to entertain me while I waited for it to all go away.

Rosemary sat at the opposite end of the couch with her legs drawn up tightly. She talked quietly and watched me.

"I just can't believe it. This just doesn't happen. . . ."

"I know, Rosemary."

"When Jon came to pick up the kids, I knew this was what it was. He didn't say anything. . . . He would have said if it was a car accident or something. I knew it had to be this. . . . I was a nervous wreck all day. I was dying to call and hear it wasn't so. . . . God, I can't believe I was just here, taking care of your kids while it was happening. It was just such a normal day till Jon called. I knew it had to be this. . . . I didn't sleep much last night. . . ."

I listened. I was glad to listen to someone else, to hear how someone else felt. I wanted to comfort her and apologize for causing her such worry.

"How did Jon react?" she asked.

"I don't know. He hasn't said much. He drove home in a hurry though. I couldn't believe hearing the SAAB screech into the driveway. He's been so good."

"You're lucky."

"Yeah."

We sat for four hours, talking when we found something to say. Even the kids were very quiet that day.

"I should go home . . . but I don't want to."

"Oh, you don't have to go. Stay till Jon gets home. It's O.K."

"Kathy called yesterday to apologize about not playing tennis. . . . I didn't tell her. I'm supposed to take care of her kids this weekend. They have been planning this weekend for so long. Her girls are so good though, they shouldn't be any trouble."

"You're going to have them all weekend?"

"Tomorrow morning till Sunday afternoon. Jon will be home."

We both found it hard to talk about the future or the past. We were both waiting in uncertainty. I left when I was sure Jon was home.

That night Jon sat on the side of my bed after the kids were asleep.

"What are you thinking?"

"Nothing," as I curled up into a tighter ball on the bed.

He massaged my back awhile silently.

"You're not up to this weekend, are you?"

"I don't know. We can't call them now. It's so late."

"I don't know if I can take care of four kids and you all at once. I'd better call them, Jenn. I'll just say something came up."

"What can you say? You'll have to tell them. . . ."

He used the phone in the kitchen where I couldn't hear.

"Kathy said it was no problem. They understood."

"What did you tell her?"

"I said you were assaulted. . . . She suggested we go over there for dinner tomorrow night and I said I'd let her know in the morning, O.K.?"

"Yeah, O.K., if we can get a sitter. What was her reaction to the assault?"

"She was relieved to hear you weren't raped. She was obviously shocked to hear about it."

"Yeah, what could she say anyway."

JOURNAL - October 17, Friday

I guess it is time to write about it. What does one say? Thoughts race on, contradicting themselves. Some sane, some not. Only the terror repeats itself constantly. Again and again. I see his face, the blue sky, a man on a walk, the explosion of all light and thought. His arm strangling me. Death. Then the knife, the walk to the thicket—scenes from a movie I didn't want to watch. But I was forced to, I had to endure, I had to survive. To survive I watched without feeling. There was nothing I could do.

CHAPTER III

Jon wanted me to sleep on Saturday. I needed the rest, I wanted the escape, but the soft bed and quiet room could not subdue my senses. My ribs still felt the knife, my neck still ached from his grip, my nose was still saturated with the stench. I was filled with the terror of how close death had been, how fragile life was. Life could be lost in an instant and it could be *my* life. Death was real. It could come even on a beautiful autumn day, with no warning, no doctor's diagnosis, no lingering in a hospital bed to say good-by and bravely face death. Death could come with no preparation. Death had spit its terror in my face and I could not forget.

"Jenn, do you feel O.K. about going to the Taylors' to-

night? We don't have to go if you're not up to it." Jon had
been quietly rubbing my back.

"It's O.K. We should go. I mean, after all it's not often
that the Taylors have an open weekend like this, with no
plans now. It's hard to catch them at home. We should take
advantage of it."

"That's true. Hadn't looked at it that way. But if you
get too tired, we can come home early. Maybe it'll help. Be
sure to tell me when we should come home though, O.K.?"

"Yeah, O.K. What time did you say we're going?" My
sense of a future was still vague and I was depending on Jon
to manage it.

"Seven-thirty. It's flexible though, whenever we get the
kids in bed. The sitter is coming at seven-thirty, O.K.?"

"Seven-thirty. O.K., three hours? I could wash my hair
. . . could . . . Are the kids napping?"

"Yeah. They'll probably wake up soon."

"Maybe I'll work a puzzle for a while."

"Don't you want to try to sleep?"

"I can't. . . . It's. . . . Hold me, Jon. Just hold me for a
minute. I love you."

"Jenn—" he stroked the head pressing into his chest—
"Jenn, I wish you could sleep."

"No, I need to get up—to do something—"

At the Taylors' that night, Kathy was still busy in the
kitchen when we arrived, and Steve was putting the girls to
bed upstairs. I said "Hello" to Kathy, then sat in the rocker
by the fire, listening to Jon talk, out in the kitchen, with
Kathy.

"Would you like a drink, Jennifer?" Kathy popped in to
ask.

"Yes, thank you. Anything would be fine."

"When Steve comes down I'll ask him to fix one of his specialties. You know how I am with drinks. Sorry we're so disorganized here. Thought dinner would be under control. Do you want a magazine or something? I just got a new garden book. I know you'll like it. It has organic-gardening hints, using insects—like you told me about the praying mantis. Where'd I put it now?"

"It's O.K., Kathy. I'm all right. I can see it another time."

"You sure? Jon's in there making the salad. I'd better . . . You can come join us. I'm using a new recipe for the chicken, hope it turns out. I know how you're not supposed to use new recipes on company but . . . Have you ever tried pumpkin bread? I made some today."

"No. Sounds good." Her chatter was exhausting me. I was finally left alone again to watch the fire and listen to the distant conversation until Steve came in with his normal exuberant welcome.

"Hi, Jennifer! Good to see you!"

"Hi," I said quietly, barely raising my head. I didn't want him to see me.

After dinner, Jon and Steve discussed work while Kathy and I tried to manage a conversation.

"Have you seen your family lately, Jenn?" Steve asked, cutting through both conversations.

"I saw my brother Dana last week. Hadn't seen him in a long time. They just moved, you know. The house—this house, well you know how Dana is about yard work, superfanatic, every blade of grass in place? Well, this yard is a riot—" My voice became animated for a moment as I tried to repeat the story the way I had told it a week before to Rosemary, but my voice suddenly dropped. "The yard is just very big."

Everyone silently waited for me to finish the story. Everyone was looking at me.

"Just a big yard—and—a mess. . . ." I dropped my head and pulled my hair in front of my face. I wanted to crawl into the pillow I held in my lap. I wanted to fade away. There was no escape. Jon finished the story of Dana's extensive complaints about the state of the yard which met average standards of gardening. The humor was lost, but the story ended with polite laughter. We left soon after that.

I went to church on Sunday to follow a familiar routine. It was something normal I could do without effort, and maybe some rational thoughts could surface there. I lost the context of the service as I silently studied people, wondering what was going on in their private lives. I wondered if I looked as different as I felt. I felt that everyone could see right through me. I felt naked. What would people think of me if they knew? I was apart from everyone. I knew it. I didn't belong. At the door, the pastor said a quick "Good morning" and turned his smile quickly to the next person.

JOURNAL - October 19, Sunday

So lonely. I feel like I am strange—a leper. How can I escape my thoughts—I want to flee from them. Sleep, but to sleep I must pass through the maze of fears, memories, details. Sleep ends and I am back again, waiting for something. Waiting for something but nothing is expected. Waiting for someone to take my thoughts away. The dishes pile up, the excuses run out. I sit and wait. Who can I talk to?

Who can help? Am I being melodramatic? Can't I just handle this myself? Forget it? Oh it is all so dumb. Such a
nightmare. But I've got to get through it, get over it not ignore it. If I have to deal with how to face people, how to
talk to friends, how to answer the phone, it is so much
harder. Where is there escape?

I remembered a conversation I had with Ava, Nigel's
Sunday-school teacher. She dropped by occasionally to see
the children as a break from her errands. The conversation I
was remembering was on a day when Ava was noticeably
distraught. A child she knew had been molested by a teenager. As Ava told the story, praising the child and the parents, it became obvious that her concerns were centered on
the teenager. She was furious with a person who could do
such a thing to an innocent child, but her fury itself seemed
the object of her anguish. "The things I'd like to do to a kid
like that! The things I'd like to do to a person who makes me
think such violent thoughts! What can become of a person, a
teenager, who would do such a thing?" I remembered her
conflicts and her anger. Perhaps she could tell me how her
mind had been quieted, perhaps she could understand my
distress. I called her, hoping that she might untangle the
web in my mind.

"Hi, Jennifer! How are you? So good to hear from you!"

"I didn't see you in church yesterday. You were away?"

"We escaped to the mountains for two whole days. My
phone has been ringing off the wall all morning. You'd
think the roof would fall in if I wasn't here to hold it up.
What's on your mind?"

"Can you come over? I need someone to talk to."

"Uh oh. Sounds like something's wrong."

"Yeah."

"In about an hour?"

"That's fine, Ava. Thanks."

I spent the hour moving chairs around in the living room, trying to decide which would be the most comfortable seating arrangement for this conversation. I didn't know what I would say to her or how she would react to anything I said. I knew I needed to be assured I wasn't alone. When she arrived, Ava sat down at the kitchen table where we usually chatted, while I fumbled to pour us some coffee.

"O.K., Jennifer. What's up?"

"Well . . ." I looked at her and knew a gradual approach wouldn't work. "O.K., Ava, catch this. I was assaulted last Wednesday. Dumb, huh?"

"Uhn-uhn. That's not dumb." She didn't accept my flippancy. I knew I was terrorized, but I didn't know if other people would view the assault as a disaster or a mishap. I wanted to be assured that there was nothing to be upset about, yet just as urgently, I wanted to be assured that I was not overreacting to something minor.

The assault was so vivid in my mind, it did not occur to me to offer her any details of the event. Though she must have been curious to know exactly what had happened, she did not ask.

"You look pretty shaken up," she continued. "How are the kids?"

"Fine." Then I understood her question. "They weren't

with me. I went for a walk—alone." I looked away to avoid encountering her reaction. *Alone. Not quite alone.*

"How are you managing the kids? It was last Wednesday?" Her mind was on the present, while mine was still tangled in the woods.

"Wednesday, yes, last Wednesday. Jon has helped so much. He stayed home from work."

"It was serious, wasn't it?" I looked at her, unable to find the reference point from which I could evaluate the situation. "I mean, it was more than just a scare, wasn't it, Jennifer?"

"I was scared. It just all keeps happening over and over."

"Some things don't disappear easily. I still have nightmares about my accident. Not at night, the nightmares that hit while I'm in the midst of mopping the floor or hanging out clothes. It's been three years and they still happen occasionally."

"I didn't know about your accident."

"I guess that was before you came here. A man was killed—the other driver."

"Oh, Ava . . ." I could understand her nightmares better than I could understand mine.

"The worst part is that I never remembered how it happened. Total blank. I remember the doubts, my fears that it was my fault. I was cleared—legally, but it was a difficult thing to live with. It was a very lonely experience. Sometimes I felt like no one could understand how I felt. I felt very alone." She spoke slowly and had been watching me as she told her story. "You feel alone, don't you?"

"I don't know. Alone sounds nice." I smiled, but she

didn't understand my humor. "I just feel like—I don't even know how to talk to people. Everything seems so far away. Everyone is in such a different world . . ."

"Have you told anyone else?"

"I talked to Pastor Duncan. He was very nice. No one else knows."

"Well, you have my word; if there's any telling, it's when you decide to." She took my hand as she continued. "Do you blame God for what happened?"

"No, not really." I didn't look at her.

"Good. Some people might."

Of course I didn't blame God, I thought. God was Creation, Beauty, the Order of Things. But if God was all powerful, all knowing, how could this happen? Was it passively observed? Was the shade pulled to avoid the sight? Was Beauty overwhelmed and as powerless as I was? Was I deserted, misguided, or manipulated by the Source of All Life? My confusion about God had to wait until more immediate concerns were sorted out.

"Jennifer, listen, any time you want to talk or just need company or if I can take the kids, you know my number. I'm glad you called me today. I hope I didn't make things worse, talking about my past."

"Oh, Ava. You've been such a help. Just to be with me."

"I'll call you in a day or so. Get some rest now and take care of yourself." I didn't know until much later that she went home and cried.

My mother called that evening.

"Did you tell her?" Jon asked when I mentioned it.

"No."

To fill the next day, Rosemary and I took the kids to a

tot lot. We avoided the secluded, private playgrounds, which we usually preferred, and found a tot lot near a shopping center. The kids played happily in the sunshine as the babies slept in their strollers by our feet.

"No one knows yet, do they?" Rosemary asked.

"Yeah. Kathy, and the pastor Jon called, and Ava know. I called Ava myself."

"But I mean your family—your mother and Michelle."

"Why?"

"They're your family. . . ."

"They don't need to know."

"I don't understand why you won't tell them."

"Rosemary—it would just hurt. Why tell someone now. I don't want to scare anyone. Why?"

"I don't know. It just seems like you're trying to protect everyone and—it's not protecting anyone. If you were in the hospital, you'd tell them. . . ."

"But I'm not and I won't. I just don't want to."

I was surprised that Rosemary didn't understand.

Construction workers passed us on their lunch break. I froze as they walked towards us. Though I tried to continue our conversation, my fears were not hidden. I couldn't trust any man. Every man, stranger or friend, was a potential rapist. I didn't know how to detect the difference or whether there was a difference. Rosemary suggested that we leave.

I had avoided any thoughts of the luncheon I had planned with a new neighbor on Wednesday. I wanted to believe I could function normally after allowing a whole week for recovery. On Wednesday morning when I found myself still dazed and confused, I didn't know how to back out graciously. I didn't want her to think our visit wasn't important to me. She had moved in during the summer, and though I had spoken to her when we had encountered each other outside, I had been too busy with summer activities to offer a firmer welcome. As I watched her children head for school one morning, I realized my days were not any less busy and if I wanted to establish a friendship I would have to stop procrastinating. On that Tuesday I had called and she enthusiastically accepted my invitation for lunch the next week.

I was up early on Wednesday, cleaning and preparing lunch, being thankful for the children's quietness so that I could concentrate on my careful preparations. If I wanted life to be normal again, I had to act as if it was.

When Sandy arrived, the children provided easy conversation and entertainment until I put them down for naps so that we could eat. Sandy had moved here from the West Coast, so we compared the differences in lifestyles and the difficulties of adjusting to the East. She was animated and warm and seemed relieved to have someone understand the changes she had to adapt to. I listened more than I usually did and filled pauses with nervous laughter to cover my serious mood.

When she left I felt a mixture of relief and loneliness in the sudden quiet. I felt my act had failed—I had not convinced myself that life was normal nor had I established a friendship with Sandy. She had not met *me;* she had met a nervous, awkward woman who had little to say. When I saw her in the yard after that luncheon, I waved and rushed on in pretense of an urgent errand.

JOURNAL - October 22, Wednesday

Where am I now? Beginning to function. Some sleep. How easily it all comes back though. The thought of VD popped up this morning. How dumb. A whole week before I thought of it. I made an appointment to see the doctor for Friday. Things are in better perspective now, I know what happened, I think I can deal with seeing a doctor now.

Rosemary's husband said he would have fought back no matter what. He would have died first. Of course, he's a man. Perhaps I could have fought back but is violence the only answer to violence? Maybe I've been too protected, maybe people should have a little tan to take the sun with. But if we are prepared for violence, we expect it. If we expect it we cannot love openly and fearlessly. It builds till there is no peace—only fear and those who take advantage of the fear. We can't prepare ourselves for the unpredictable.

Riding to the doctor's on Friday, I carefully examined the occupants of passing cars. Looking for him. He could be lurking anywhere, waiting to strike again. He had become a part of me, always lurking in my shadow. Or did part of me belong to him? He had taken part of my soul and I was left vulnerable. There was a real bond between us that was harder to admit. A bond in intimacy, a bond in secrecy. He was the only witness to the event. I preferred the more mystical thoughts because through witchcraft he ceased being a normal person.

I found myself thinking about many past episodes with men, where I had been intimidated, felt guilty, felt used. Suddenly there was one relief—*this time, he* would be punished. This time I would not have to sit back powerlessly and assume the blame. This time I had more powerful forces on my side. This time—if he could be found.

The doctor had scheduled my appointment earlier than his normal hours, and for once he was on time, so I was spared waiting in a roomful of chattering pregnant women. When I had made the appointment, I said I was sexually assaulted and wanted VD tests. I didn't know what was involved. I thought it would be a simple blood test. The nurse ushered me back to the examining room.

"When was your last period? Is there a chance of pregnancy?"

"My period came . . . afterwards." I just wanted a VD test. Of his two nurses, the terser one was on duty that day, but she shed her normal efficient airs and seemed very concerned.

"You'll need to take off your clothes from the waist down. Here is a sheet for you." Just a VD test. Not all this, just a test.

"I . . . I . . . wasn't really raped. . . . I mean I could have VD but . . ."

She stood at the door and looked at me, trying to understand what I was saying. Couldn't she understand I didn't want an exam? It didn't occur to me that I didn't have to comply or that I could talk to the doctor first and at least understand what had to be done to check for VD. I submitted and took off my clothes.

I sat numbly waiting for the doctor in my draped sheet, hiding nothing, feeling like a body again. "It has to be done," I told myself. The nurse returned with the doctor and stood silently near my feet. The doctor was very serious and quiet during the examination. No big smile or chatter this time. I escaped back to Biology 102 lab. I wanted to get up and join them in their examination of the microbe under the draped sheet. I hoped the poor thing was properly anesthetized to endure such an ordeal.

"Are you O.K.?" I hated the nurse for intruding on my biology class. I hated her for reminding me I was a person.

When the exam was over, the doctor said he wanted to talk to me in his office. I sat up and began to dress, wanting to disappear, anything to escape quietly. *Just tell me if I have VD, that's all. Don't even remember my name.* Why did I go to a doctor who knew me?—the one who had delivered my babies and had seen me in glowing motherhood only a few months earlier. How could I go into his office and face him? I had to. I had to have some help even if he thought I was neurotic. I didn't know what to say. I couldn't even look at him, and he waited for me to speak. He handed me a slip for the blood test and said where and when to have it done. I felt so desperate.

"I can't sleep. I'm so nervous all the time. I'm still breast-feeding the baby. Is there anything that can help?" *Something to erase it all from my memory. Something to make me normal again.*

"Medicine isn't the cure for everything. There is a lot of pain that just takes time and family support. There is a mild tranquilizer I can give you. It's not very strong, but it should help some and won't hurt the baby. I'm glad to hear you're still nursing." I put the prescription and lab slip in my purse and stood up.

"Thank you." I felt his eyes follow me to the door.

JOURNAL - October 24, Friday

I feel like I've run out of things to say. It happened, what more is there? But the feelings won't leave. I wish I could cry, faint, vomit, sneeze, anything besides stare at the wall. How can such a stupid incident paralyze me like this? It's over. Why won't it go away!

That night after a week and a half of suspended time, Jon felt we should ask my family for some help with the kids.

"Jenn, I think I should ask your mom to come for the weekend. We can't hide it from her forever, the way things are going. We both need a break and it would give me more time to be with you."

"Yeah. I guess you're right. I wish we didn't have to. . . . I wonder how she'll take it? . . . Be gentle when you tell her."

I knew how the news had affected Rosemary; her world was very shaken. I didn't want to project my shock into other people's lives, least of all my mother's. But Jon needed support too. He needed a break, and sooner or later my mother would be aware I was avoiding her or would be exposed to my retreating disposition.

My mother came immediately.

"Jenn . . ." It was a mixed statement and question that carried the weight of her hour-long drive in darkness.

"Hi, Mom." I didn't move from the chair as she came in. "I'm O.K. Just very tired." I dismissed the most obvious questions, trying to avoid anxiety during the evening.

"Oh, Jenn—you look tired. Are the kids in bed already?

I hurried, thinking I could help get them tucked in. . . . I forget how capable Jon is. . . ."

Nothing was said about why we were together that evening. There was some quiet talk before we turned our stares to the TV. When Bergman's *Virgin Spring* came on, my mother chose not to watch and went to bed. The movie did not create unbearable repulsion in me as it had in the past. This time I did not look away during the rape and murder of the young girl. I was reassured by the recognition of the horror.

My mother created the quiet atmosphere we hoped for during the weekend, reading to the kids in her room and answering their demands. While the kids were napping on Saturday, I went to my mother's room to talk to her. I didn't know what Jon had told her. I assumed he had said simply that I had been assaulted; he didn't know much more than that himself. I felt I needed to tell her more about what happened.

"Sorry we didn't call earlier. I thought we could handle this. You know, no big deal, just a bad experience. Rosemary was baby-sitting the kids that day and I went out to the lake to take pictures. It was such a pretty day. I—"

"When was it? How long ago?"

"A week ago Wednesday. Nearly two weeks now."

"But I just called you last week, didn't I?" There was pain in her voice that I didn't want to acknowledge.

"You called last Monday."

"Yes, Monday. I thought it was Monday. . . ."

"Anyway, I didn't want to tell anyone. It just shook me up and it's so hard to get any rest with the kids and all. It's been so nice today—so nice and quiet."

"Did you nap?"

"I lay down for a while. It was all so weird, with the police and all. They were really nice though, not like you hear all these stories. . . . I was just glad to be alive—he had a knife. . . . It was just such an ordinary day. . . ."

"You don't have to talk about it now if you don't want to. Why don't you try to sleep?"

I wasn't sure how much I would have told her if she had let me go on talking. I wanted her to understand, but I didn't want her to worry that I couldn't take care of myself.

"Michelle said she'd like to take a day off work to come over. She's upset too, of course."

"Michelle? Oh, that's nice of her to offer." I hadn't thought about whether Mom would tell anyone, but my sister-in-law was an obvious person to be told. Mom lived with Michelle and my brother. Of course, she'd be upset. I had thought of calling her soon after the attack, but I couldn't. I wished I had told her directly, but I was glad she knew.

It was hard for me to confess to my family that I needed help. Even Michelle had picked up the family attitude that "Jenn can handle anything." Big, tough Jenn . . . I wanted to keep that image.

We didn't mention the subject again that weekend.

JOURNAL - October 27, Monday

I am beginning to feel better, the days seem possible. Still so nervous, weak knees, upset stomach. There are breaks between thoughts of it now. It would certainly make me feel better if the police caught him. It could be a long time. I should try to write things down in case I must recount it all later but I'm not up to that yet—no, it wouldn't be worth it. It would certainly be nice for everything to be back to normal but it is only a matter of time. Hopefully I'll be able to absorb myself in Christmas projects soon.

My babes were increasingly my escape. They were unaware that a change had taken place in the household. With them I could forget the changes also. I cuddled them and played with them at every opportunity. I had the time for them and the need for their closeness. Nigel was just beginning to verbalize thoughts, and we both enjoyed our discussions of why Winnie-the-Pooh always wore a red shirt and where the water went when it went down the drain. His explanations were always more interesting than mine. Colin was beginning to get around on his own, to explore his world and provided constant entertainment. I didn't look forward to their naptimes as I once did. I didn't crave the private moments that I once treasured. By four-thirty each day Nigel and I would sit on the couch watching for Jon. To shorten that last half hour of the day, we had a game of who would see his car first. Jon and I still went to bed as soon as the kids were asleep. We lay quietly and cuddled, watching TV till I was lulled to sleep.

On the fourteenth day, Jon had a meeting that prevented his five-o'clock homecoming. To avoid the empty waiting I drove to Michelle's for supper. Michelle had been a close friend long before she married my brother, before she even knew him, and we had never broken the high-school habit of talking and laughing together long into the night. My mother and brother would be there to share the evening too. I hoped this could be an escape back to life as it was before.

During supper, however, the candles hardly flickered in the still air. The laughter was muted, the conversation subdued.

"Have you heard from your folks, Michelle?" I asked.

"Um, yeah. They're fine. Dad's still working, of course. I mean he keeps saying he's going to retire, you know. . . . Mom's into stuff, you know, her clubs and stuff. . . . They're fine. . . ."

"I saw Mrs. Jackson in town the other day, Jennifer," Mom interjected during the pause. "You remember her, don't you? Your Sunday-school teacher? She asked about you."

"Oh. What did you say?"

"Oh, I said you were doing fine, of course. Showed her pictures of the boys and she said they were so good-looking."

No one knew how to continue that topic either. I felt responsible for the awkwardness around me, I was still a stone pillar disguised in a warm body. I was still unable to respond to feeling, so there was no hope of interacting, but we spent the time trying.

"How about a game of cards?" Mom didn't wait for an answer. "I'll clear the table. Marc, can you find the cards?"

For a moment Michelle and I were alone. She leaned towards me. "Jenn . . . ?" Her voice was quiet and close.

"Mom told me of your offer to help," I said quickly as I drew back from her. "Thank you. . . ."

"Jenn . . . I just thought . . . I could still take off a day from work. I'd like to if . . ."

"It's O.K., Michelle. It's really nice of you but it's O.K."

"The cards are all set up whenever you guys are ready," Marc called from the den.

Michelle sat for a moment as I got up. "Coming?"

"Jenn? . . ." I paused but didn't reply. ". . . Yeah, I'm coming."

During the game, Mom's conversation was supported by Marc's occasional replies. I studied my cards and listened but was aware of Michelle's unusual silence. She was restless and distracted and I avoided her eyes. Marc uncomfortably watched each of us. When a second game was suggested, Michelle looked at me, seemed ready to speak, then turned to Marc.

"I've really had enough. I'm going to bed. I've got a headache. . . ."

"Oh, Michelle, I—I guess it's time for me to get home anyway."

Michelle didn't reply but ran upstairs. I had never seen her hold back emotions before.

"Marc, tell Michelle I'm sorry."

"Jenn, she's just tired. It wasn't you."

"Yes, it was. I'm sorry," and I gathered my sleepy babes into the car and backed out of the driveway.

By the time I reached the highway the children were both asleep. The highway at night did not provide distractions from the thoughts floating aimlessly in my mind. *I should have talked to Michelle. She wanted to talk, to have a private talk, but what could I have told her? Surely she didn't want to hear the details.* My thoughts of Michelle vanished as suddenly the grotesque face appeared before me saying "Suck it!" My whole body was electrified with rage. The darkness outside and the road ahead disappeared behind the vividness of the image. I instinctively accelerated to escape it. Suddenly it was dark and quiet again and I trembled with fear. I had never felt such anger. I had never lost control of my emotions and I was so frightened by that moment of rage that I buried it where it smoldered for months before rising again in volcanic eruptions.

The next day, with emotions under control, I concentrated on Michelle's hurt feelings. I carefully planned my words of apology: *Hi, I'm really sorry about last night. I really appreciated your offer for help, but it's been very hard for me to talk about it. I hope we can get together soon about it.*

I wanted to say, "I didn't realize it was so important to you," but when I called her at work I couldn't say any of it.

"Hi, Michelle. I'm sorry . . ."

"Oh, it's O.K. I'm not mad at you."

"No, Michelle, you should be. I . . ."

"It was just a frustrating evening. I'd had a bad day. It's O.K."

Tears choked my words. "I'm sorry to call you at work. . . ." Poor Michelle, what could she say there at her desk at work. ". . . It's not you, please understand, Michelle, it's not you. . . ." The words disappeared in tears. I couldn't hang up; I needed to tell her.

"It's O.K., Jenn . . . Really." Her voice was shaky, too.

My sobs increased. "I'm sorry . . . you're at work . . . I'm sorry. I better let you go. I didn't mean this. . . ."

"It's O.K. I'll talk to you later, O.K.? I understand."

The tears that took two weeks to come continued after I hung up. My sobs turned to shaking and I sat down to get my thoughts together. I felt totally confused and lost. I wanted to understand what I was feeling, why my mind wouldn't think the way I wanted it to.

Rosemary's call pulled me out of my private torment. She called almost daily to see how I was.

"Oh, Rosemary. Everything is so crazy. Why is everything so mixed up?"

"Jenn, I really think you should try talking to someone. A neighbor of mine used to be involved with some group that worked with rape victims. I couldn't find anything in the directory but I'm sure the Women's Clearing House would know. That's what they are for. You know, if you talked to another victim, or someone who knew about sexual assault, I'm sure it would help. My neighbor was really concerned about rape victims. I wish she still lived here. . . ."

"Maybe you're right, but what could they say anyway . . . maybe another victim though. But what if I found out I'm just crazy. . . . I really should be able to handle this myself. I . . ."

"It wouldn't hurt to find out what's available."

"It might . . . I'm just taking this all too seriously. . . . I wasn't hurt. What would I say anyway?"

"Jennifer, you've got to take the risk. How much can you lose? Just call and say you want to talk to another victim."

"O.K. . . . Do you know the number?"

"It just happens that I have it right here. Are you going to call now?"

"Yeah." She pushed at the right moment. I was feeling lost enough to grope. I called the Clearing House.

"Hello, I was assaulted a few weeks ago and I was

wondering if you had any way of getting me in touch with another victim that I could talk to."

The woman at the Clearing House didn't treat the request as absurd. "Let me get you in touch with someone who can help you. Can I have her call you in a few minutes?"

A few minutes later the phone rang.

"Hello. This is Doris with the Rape Crisis Center. I was told you called and would like to talk to someone. How are you doing?"

"I . . . well, I'm O.K. I guess. I thought maybe if I could talk to someone, another victim . . . it's been two weeks. . . . I . . . I don't know."

"It sounds like you're still having a rough time about it."

"I guess."

"Have you been able to talk about it to anyone?"

"My husband knows about it. . . ."

"I think I know about your case from the newspaper. At the lake?"

"It was in the paper. . . . It looked pretty weird in the paper but I guess that was me."

"So it's been reported to the police then. Do they have any suspect on it?"

"No."

"Can you tell me how you feel about it now?"

"I don't know. . . . It just won't go away. I thought it might help if I could talk to another victim."

"It sounds like it's hard for you to talk about it. Maybe we should start with some practical matters. Did you see a doctor?"

"Yes . . . I took care of that. Well, I was a little slow. I feel so dumb that I didn't even think of VD till a week later. I went to my doctor then and he did the VD tests."

"Good, but you should be checked for VD again after six weeks. The Public Health Department will do it for you. I can recommend a professional counselor who works with rape victims if you feel you'd like to talk to her. She is very good and works with our center, so you might consider making an appointment with her. Her name is Margot Salzman and let me give you her phone number too."

"I'm not really the therapy type. . . . I mean I don't really believe that's necessary. It's just a matter of time, I'm sure." I valued the privacy of my thoughts; I didn't need to hear anyone else's opinion of them. Talking about private matters to a stranger seemed a strange way to resolve problems. If I couldn't resolve conflicts myself, what could a stranger offer? At this point the thought of a therapist who might delve into my private life was very threatening.

"You seem to be having a hard time talking about it on the phone. Would it be easier if I came over to see you?"

"Maybe so. I guess—yes."

I sat back in bed and thought about the conversation. The back of an envelope held doodles and notes from the call. Professional counselor . . . phone numbers I forgot the significance of . . . VD tests in six weeks. I thought the VD question was settled. The doctor said the tests were negative; Doris said I needed more tests. I reached for *Our Bodies, Ourselves*, but it was only concerned about diagnosis from symptoms. The possibility of oral infection had not been mentioned, but I hadn't told anyone that detail either.

My throat was raw and aching. I didn't want to think the possibility still existed.

Though I didn't know what to expect from Doris, I was glad she was coming over. Telephones weren't my media. I couldn't deal with long pauses or see reactions which are a part of face-to-face conversations. Jon called it my telephobia.

My day centered around the expected visit. It was an event in my uneventful days. It was a hope for an explanation, for an ending of my confusion. I needed someone who could do more than just listen to me say nothing. I was waiting at the door when she knocked and I ushered her into the den. The den was our most private room, farthest from household noise and distractions. Two walls were lined with bookshelves and a bed; a straight chair and a card table filled the opposite corner. I sat on the bed with my back against the headboard. Doris chose the chair and put a notebook on the table beside her. Her soft face was defined by eyes that searched as though trying to perceive a far-off object. She spoke very softly and she was very pregnant.

"When is the baby due?"

"Any day now." She smiled. "I'm ready."

Such a short time ago my mind and body had been filled with the anticipation of a new baby. Such a short time so many worlds away. I would have preferred discussing the imminent birth—the birth that could occur that night or the next day. I couldn't understand why she chose to be with me at such a time.

"Can you tell me about it now?" Her pregnancy did not seem to concern her.

I methodically recounted how I happened to be at the

lake, what I was doing there, how beautiful the weather was, "Suddenly there was an arm around my neck . . . the trees . . . I . . . the trees . . ." I could feel it all happening again. The small room had expanded to endless lonely woods and I was falling. . . .

"You seem very tense, talking about it. You're pulling your bedspread apart." I pulled my dazed stare down to my hands. The bedspread was damp and wrinkled where I'd been clutching it. My hands were cold and wet. My neck hurt but I smiled at the release of tension.

"I can't even go to the mailbox." *Isn't that dumb? You laugh too. It's really dumb, isn't it?* Her eyes weren't smiling.

"It's not surprising. It was a tremendous shock."

"But how long does it take? When will it go away?"

She was listening. *Answers, please, some answers. Please make it all go away. Tell me when I can wake up from this.*

"It varies from victim to victim. With some victims it lingers longer. Others resolve it more quickly. It helps to talk about it."

"But other victims . . . people don't go to pieces like this. . . . Why won't it go away?"

"Talking about it is the best thing. You still haven't told me the details." She had turned it back on me. For a moment I had dreamed, for a moment I was reaching. . . . I needed some answers.

"I'm sorry to bother you with forms, but I need some information. Can you tell me if there was penetration? . . . You know what I mean by penetration?" My quizzical look was for the basis of the question, not the definition of the word. "The State's attorney needs to have that information."

I didn't know what a State's attorney was. I envisioned a man sitting in the state capitol, collecting statistics on crime. I had not thought through the process as far as a trial. I was only waiting for the police to catch the man, for it to be done with. If it was an essential question, why hadn't the police gotten that information? But she had a form she needed to complete.

"Well, it wasn't like . . . like intercourse." I couldn't give the details. I couldn't explain why I wasn't sure if there was penetration. "No, there wasn't penetration. He didn't penetrate me." It didn't matter, it was only a statistic. That wasn't the crime he committed; put me in the miscellaneous-crime column.

"Can you tell me the sexual details?"

"No." I didn't even consider the question.

"Well, you have to talk about it sometime." She raised one eyebrow to emphasize her words.

"I have . . . to the police. That's all I need to tell." My jaw tensed at being pushed. I didn't have to tell her anything and was glad I was able to make a firm decision. It was the first concrete thought in two weeks.

Our conversation ended and I went to my room to lie down. Jon came in and asked how it went.

"O.K., I guess."

And Doris went home to have her baby.

JOURNAL - November 2, Sunday

It is obvious now that recovery is a long, slow process. I still have new feelings, new reactions but I am beginning to feel like I can function somewhat. I'm tired of asking for help. I don't know what I want now, I feel empty. It is like a gash and while the blood was gushing it was easier to ask for help. Now the gash is festering and I can't reach it or even see it to see how serious it is. If I can't see it, it'll go away seems the easiest way. I want someone to know what I need, someone to help me know what I need. Nobody has any answers.

CHAPTER IV

ALREADY the holiday season was beginning to creep up on us. The personal touches to Christmas were important to us, so we usually began work on projects early in the fall.

This year our cards had not been produced on the October schedule. We were already behind. I tried to work on a design, to think of some happy greeting. I wasn't feeling creative and was not ready for Christmas cheer. The inspiration would have to wait until the decorations began to appear, when the aura of midwinter filled the air. Meanwhile I stayed home behind locked doors and cleaned my house.

While my time was occupied by my children and routine chores, my existence revolved around Jon and Rosemary. They were my only contacts with thoughts and feelings. I waited out many days with Rosemary. We talked about violence and crime, about my encounter and about her feelings. I couldn't talk about my feelings because I didn't know them. I was determined to bury the incident. It all would fade with time if I could just wait it out. I wanted the earth to stand still until I understood its arrangements. Jon tried to protect me from avoidable stress. He answered the phone, he did the shopping and would come home to tuck me in bed. With Jon and Rosemary to hide behind, I tried to secure myself against the world. I was a soldier under siege, too determined to keep back the unknown enemy to realize the extent of my wounds. Time wasn't on my side.

Ava stopped by or called each week. I didn't have to pretend with her that I wasn't nervous and upset, but we didn't talk about the crime. I knew she would listen if I wanted to talk, but I appreciated her patience in waiting for me to be ready. She was a welcome break to my dreary days. I needed her constant reassurances that I was a special person.

I continued to go to math class with Rosemary, who drove regularly now. At class breaks Rosemary and I always sat alone, avoiding classmates' discussions. I still saw every male as a threat and every female as vulnerable.

Evenings with Jon were spent watching TV or going to bed early, but our frenzied sex life had abated. With all its intensity, it did not reassure me that I was still desirable. It reassured me that Jon cared and loved me in spite of it. I found nakedness repulsive. I cringed if I saw the reflection of my body in the mirror. I changed clothes quickly and privately. Jon's nakedness upset me to the degree that I deviously avoided his presence until I knew that he was under

the covers. I tried many subtle hints and joking remarks before my night of hysteria that got the message across to him.
Bedtime became a time of tension for both of us.

JOURNAL - November 13, Thursday
It's normal now. I wonder if it even happened. Just nothing
more to think about. Wonder if he'll ever be caught? It
hardly seems so at this point unless he strikes again. How
horrible if he struck again, if he killed someone. Somehow
I'd be a part of it—that I didn't stop him? that I escaped? I
hope he's caught before he really hurts someone. It seems
only a matter of time.

As soon as a new minister was chosen for our church, the
church council held a small reception for him. Though he
would not be assuming his pastoral duties until January, I
felt both obligated to go and curious to meet him. I hoped I
could listen and be unnoticed in the crowd. Wearing a long,
loose dress that covered everything except my hands and
face, I still felt very exposed. I wanted to hide behind Jon,
but I was approached by friendly women inquiring about
the baby and admiring my dress. I hoped my polite smiles
were enough to support the conversation. A very talkative
member of our church joined the conversation and soon the
other women, one by one, drifted away. Though her chatter
was often a challenge to endure, she was my refuge that
evening. She didn't require any response from me and no
one else had a chance to tap in.

Later, when we all gathered into a circle to talk together, I sat on the floor, trying to clutch Jon unobtrusively.
I sat very close to him, my leg touching his. I fidgeted and

avoided looking at anyone. The rug was my center of attention. I tried to hide my discomfort and even started to say
something, but as soon as I felt everyone's eyes turn to me, I
cut my comment short and pressed harder against Jon.

That night I curled to the edge of my bed, clutching
my shoulders.

"Is something wrong, Jenn?" Jon asked.

"I'm so ugly. . . ." I would have preferred not to speak
of the thoughts that were on my mind, but they were too
strong to hide that night.

"Jennifer! Why do you say that? You . . ."

"No . . . not ugly . . . not just ugly. I'm so nothing . . .
so weak . . . so dirty."

"Jenn, don't. . . ."

"Just all those people tonight. I just didn't want them
to look at me. I just wanted to be a room fixture, where I
could listen, observe . . . just be there so I wasn't alone . . .
but no one could talk to me or see me. . . ."

"Oh, Jenn, I'm sorry I pushed you to go. I should have
known . . ."

"No . . . no, Jon. It's not them. I just can't pretend."

JOURNAL - November 17, Monday

I feel like the subject is closed. I guess I don't want to talk
to anyone. It doesn't seem like most people have anymore to
offer than they have already given, and some I just don't
feel like talking to anymore. I'd like to talk more I think, but
there's not much I can tell. How long can I tell the same
people the same stuff? I wish Jon could understand. He is
the one I wish I could really talk to. It's not easy for him either but he seems the only one that can make me feel good.
I really need a lot of compliments and pampering just now.

JOURNAL - November 18, Tuesday

"You're gonna get it! You're really gonna get it!" and she ran home screaming to Mommy and Mommy was really mad too. "Boy, is he gonna get it!" and Mommy kissed her and stroked her hair and gradually she realized he wasn't gonna get it and the hurt went deeper and she realized not even Mommies could heal every hurt and she cried harder.

JOURNAL - November 19, Wednesday

It's because no one knows anyone else. No one knows their neighbor's lives. We must make quick judgments, assumptions. Even our families are distant, even they must make assumptions. We can hide anything from anyone. No one has the ability, time, energy to even try to understand other people. Faulkner could never write about suburbia—there is nothing here. Blank faces over plastic cups of instant coffee. Who would Emily be? An old lady that lives alone and dies alone and no one to write her obituary.

Spending Thanksgiving with Jon's family had never been decided, it was just assumed. We hadn't seen his folks since July and of course they wanted to see their growing grandsons. I felt the pressure of family obligations, but I didn't want to go.

I sat on the floor, staring out the window at the dark trees against the gray sky, as I debated telling Jon how I felt. He sat near me, reading. I hadn't been discussing my feelings with Jon. It was easier to say nothing than to try to explain.

"How long are we going to stay in Massachusetts?"

I was still staring out the window. He began to answer the question before he realized I wasn't listening.

"I don't want to go. . . . I don't want to go anyplace. I don't even want to do anything or see anyone. . . . When is it going to go away? I want to take a long vacation and leave me at home. . . ." Tears streamed down my face, but I wasn't sobbing. My voice was quiet. I was talking to the trees, pleading with them to release me from my imprisonment.

I had tried to deny the depth of my fears, but a trip would mean venturing away from the little security I found in my own home. I was afraid to leave my familiar retreats. I would be among people who didn't even know what had happened. How could I hold up my mask for days?

"Jenn . . . Jenn . . . We don't have to go," Jon tried to tell me, trying to break into my pleading with the trees. I finally heard him and felt ashamed. I was pushing my dilemma onto Jon and knew he would accept it. He would make the decision for me. He would tell his family we weren't going and cover the situation. He would allow me my escape, but I couldn't escape feelings of letting the family down. I'd be depriving them of seeing the kids, keeping the kids from a nice holiday, preventing Jon from seeing his family. It wasn't an escape.

As I regained control of my mind, we reached a compromise. We would stay for only one night and Jon would explain to his mother. It would be a long drive, but we could meet our obligations and I'd only have to pretend for a short period. It didn't erase my anxieties, but it turned an impossible situation into a merely difficult one.

On the six-hour drive I was thankful for my bladder's

endurance. At each rest stop I stayed in the security of our locked car, rather than go alone to the toilet.

The house in Massachusetts was in a quiet area. There was enough space between houses to make each residence whole and independent. Jon's grandmother's house backed up to a deep woods where we usually enjoyed walks, discovering woodland flowers, resting to dream on large rock outcroppings. On my first visit there, in the spring before we were married, we found a beautiful, perfect purple trillium. It became a special symbol and the symbol became part of my wedding ring the next year. It was a beautiful serene place to visit any time of year.

On that Thanksgiving the woods did not beckon me. I spent as much time in our room as I could, using the kids or exhaustion from the long drive as an excuse.

In the evening Jon found me sitting on our bed. I stood to hug him. Behind him was a window and I watched a car's headlights on the road beyond. As it passed I started shaking. It had been a tense day but it was more than that. Did I dare tell Jon my silly fears? Did I dare admit my childish imagination?

"Jon, you know someone could just drive past here and shoot us. We're so visible in front of the window. It happens." My fear of sudden, instant death was still very alive.

He didn't laugh—"Poor baby. I know"—and he hugged me tighter.

"I'm not a baby," I whispered teasingly.

I lay down on the bed, with Jon sitting beside me, and remembered the morning six years earlier when he sat on that bed to awaken me the first time I'd slept in that room.

It was Thanksgiving then too, when we had come up together to announce our engagement.

JOURNAL - November 27, Thanksgiving

I certainly am a crabby, unfriendly person these days. I can't seem to enjoy people at all. People seem to complain so much and listen so little. I don't care about anyone except my own. Not a very good feeling at Christmas. Even with Jon I get so irritable and crabby whenever I get tense. Maybe there is something to the idea of being possessed by evil—I am a grouch when I don't want to be. I can't help it. Maybe it just depends on which is in control.

We cut our Thanksgiving trip short so that I could attend a meeting on Saturday. I had received a call in November from the Rape Crisis Center inviting me to join a series of rap sessions for rape victims. I had told them I would come, but as the day approached I grew apprehensive. My attempts to forget it, to dispel it, to deal with my reactions alone, were not succeeding. I needed to do something to help me deal with my feelings. I needed to hear how other women dealt with it. I had to go.

Entering the brick office building with large recessed windows, my breath was stilled by the emptiness. Glass doors enclosed the hall at each end and between were only closed, numbered doors lined up on each side of the elevators. I could not even hear my footsteps on the thick carpet. I welcomed the security of the empty elevator but was in constant fear that the door would open to reveal a waiting person. The stillness followed me down the hall again as I followed the numbers to 315. I took a deep breath, pushed back my hair, and slowly opened the door.

"Hello, I'm Carol. Are you Jennifer?" A thin, red-haired woman reached out to me warmly. Her low voice identified her as the woman who had called me to be there. Carol and one other victim were there. "I guess this is our group today. None of the other victims could come this week, but I felt we should start anyway."

I had hoped that I could sit back and listen during the session, but the intimacy of this small group seemed threatening. I found myself eyeing the other victim carefully. Karen looked so normal, acted so normal. I could have met her anyplace. She was attractive, well-dressed, middle class, articulate, but she had been through it too. Though she had been raped eight years earlier, she explained that this was the first opportunity she had had to talk about it. Since it had happened before her marriage, she had not even told her husband.

So much of my loneliness was the emptiness of knowing of no one else who had gone through this. I had no mirrors, no comparisons, no identity. It happened in the newspapers, but the victims were nameless and disappeared after the papers went to press. They were a different kind of woman, not part of my world, not women I knew.

The spotlight turned quickly on me; since I was the recent victim, I was in the midst of it. I tried to squirm out of the light, explaining that I wasn't really a rape victim, not like Karen. It didn't work. They didn't care where he had put his penis. I felt naked and vulnerable and defenseless. I didn't want to tell them my weak spots, where they could hurt me if they turned on me. I wanted to control what people thought of me. If I didn't say what I was thinking, they couldn't judge my thoughts. I needed to trust these people; they were there to help, but I needed time to be able to trust them. Jon was the only one I trusted, but he had no more answers than I did. I struggled with my fears for the two-hour session, but I knew I would return.

Jon and I had known for months that he would have to make a business trip to California in December. Originally, before things had changed, we had all planned to go. I loved California, I wanted to go away with Jon, I didn't want to be left alone, but as the trip approached we had to face the reality. I wasn't able to enjoy much and the expense wasn't inconsiderable. I didn't think I could leave the little security I found in my house for strange motels. Camping was out of the question. We gave up the idea and I tried not to think about how I would survive a week without Jon.

JOURNAL - December 2, Tuesday

It makes me furious that I cannot enjoy the things I usually do. I don't want to see my family. I don't want to go to California. The thought of going to the San Diego Zoo where it was so beautiful two years ago—such a lovely walk alone all day—now I am afraid to go anywhere alone. I am imprisoned—the victim is incarcerated, the assailant is free and satisfied. I should hate the assailant but I hate myself and those close to me. I should feel innocent but I feel guilty. Why can't I get anything straight?

I did not mention Jon's trip at the next meeting of the rap group. I was less conspicuous because of the three added victims who joined the group, and I was granted the privacy of my thoughts that I sought. I was allowed to sit back and listen to how the other victims thought and felt. Debby had been raped six years earlier on a date and, like Karen, had not reported it to anyone. Leila, a victim of three years ago, a young mother when it happened, was raped by a stranger. I felt an identity with her situation, though I was intimidated by her beauty and confidence. She was where I wanted to be. Had she possibly been as devastated by the attack on her as I was? I wanted her to tell me how to cope, how to put myself back together, but I still could not admit how apart I was. I dared to ask her, "How long does it take? How long did you feel the effects?"

"I couldn't go out alone for over a year. I had to see a psychiatrist about it long after it happened. I'm still scared." Was she just saying that to give me plenty of time? I wanted to believe that she suffered too and had come back a beautiful person. I *didn't* want to believe that anyone could suffer from it for so long.

"I learned a lot from it all, though. . . . Really." She added, "You can come out of it a stronger, more complete person."

Maybe . . . maybe some people do. It carried a resonance of hope. I tucked her statement away for future use.

The third new member, Marylee, was a teenager who had been raped a week after I was. She was very quiet and I was afraid to assume she was suffering as much as I was.

I could retreat more easily in the larger group and was more comfortable with the discussion. We talked about the crime of rape rather than specific cases, but the story of Leila's trial came out. Her assailant had been sentenced to five years, but not for rape, because of a technicality. A discussion of the rape laws ensued, of the technicalities involved. I was confused by comments which didn't fit my understanding of rape. "He can stick his penis anywhere, but if it touches the vagina, it's suddenly rape." I was embarrassed to voice my ignorance openly and felt uneasy about some of the implications. "The difference in sentencing between sodomy and rape is unreal." It hadn't occurred to me that the difference mattered. Afterwards, I waited as everyone was leaving, hoping to catch Carol alone.

"Can you tell me the legal definition of rape?"

"Yes. I have it here." She paged through her notebook. "Penetration, however slight, by force or threat of force, against the will and consent of the other person."

"Uh . . . what does it mean 'however slight'?"

"Why?" She was probing. She was an anxious listener.

"I'm just confused about it . . . some stuff said today . . . I didn't understand."

"Is the confusion about what happened to you?"

"No. I don't know . . . It's O.K. I'm just confused."

"I'm not sure of the technical limit of what constitutes rape except that it is any contact of the victim's vagina by his penis." Her eyes were fixed on me as she paused. "Did the police charge him with rape?"

"No, sodomy and assault. That's what I told them about."

"That's what you told them?" Carol was very careful in phrasing her questions and statements. She seemed to consider things very thoroughly before she spoke.

"That was the significant part of it."

"Did you tell the police all the details?"

"I . . . yes, well . . . I don't know . . . He kept telling

me he wasn't going to rape me but he . . . he was trying every method of masturbating. It's not important now. . . . I'm just trying to get it straight in my head. It doesn't matter."

"It bothers me if you feel you didn't tell everything to the police. Is there anything else you didn't tell them?'"

"No, just little things I've thought of, nothing important."

I had to get home to be with Jon before he left for California. I didn't want to think about it anymore.

JOURNAL - December 6, Saturday

Wish I could identify my feelings now. Had rap session at the Center this morning. Jon is leaving for California tomorrow morning. Really depressed, yet numb. I don't want to talk about it, I just want this week to be over. I really need Jon. I don't even know what I want or don't want anymore. I just don't care.

We took Jon to the airport on Sunday morning. Nigel was in love with airplanes and his excitement over every plane was infectious. Jon boarded his plane and we stayed to watch it take off. The kids distracted me from the anxieties of his departure. He had to go. I could handle it. I'd survived by myself many times before. It was difficult leading Nigel back to the car. Carrying Colin in the backpack, I still needed more arms and more mobility to keep Nigel under control. When we got into the car I sat for a moment, collecting my nerves for the drive home.

We drove to the parking-lot toll booth totally unaware that we could have become a permanent fixture there. We had parked for four mintues past an hour, which meant I had to pay for an extra half hour. I was eighteen cents short. The toll taker was well trained in her role. She recited her lines perfectly even though they were not related to the situation or what I was trying to say to her. She said I would have to return to the "ticket office of the airlines which was serving me in order to get a waiver of the eighteen cents." I couldn't understand the directions much less consider maneuvering my two babes back into the terminal again—even if I could have moved my car! "Please move your car to the middle lane of traffic." She said it at least twice. What middle lane? There was only one lane. I couldn't move my car anywhere with a closed gate in front and a line of cars in back. I was in tears and nearing hysteria but refused to try to cooperate. Cars lined up behind me, honking. Just as I began to get out of my car to walk down the line, looking for a driver impatient enough to give me eighteen cents, the manager arrived. When I explained again the four minutes and eighteen cents, he took my collection of change and let me drive out. After that beginning to my five days of self-survival, I wasn't sure how far I would make it.

JOURNAL - December 7, Sunday

I'm almost convinced that woman was a machine. I've never met anyone so inhuman! She didn't even look at me, just recited her recorded message, not listening. When I said anything she merely stopped speaking then backed up to the beginning of her sentence. How unreal! For eighteen cents! God! For four minutes even. How to rebuild my confidence in humanity. Either I've totally cracked (which I came near to in any case) or she was and since she was in the position of power I was convinced for the moment at least that I was!

I spent that night at Michelle's to avoid emptiness. I thought about the absurd woman at the airport all afternoon, but it was 9 P.M. before I was able to tell anyone. I was afraid it sounded so absurd my family would conclude I'd cracked. I wasn't sure I hadn't. I was relieved when they believed me and laughed at her.

I went home the next day because I couldn't avoid the emptiness.

Monday night Carol called to ask if I wanted to talk about the matter I brought up at rap session.

"Do you think you could talk to the police again? I talked to a lawyer about the legal implications of your going back to the police now. If something should come up at a trial that wasn't part of your original statement . . . Obviously it would have been better if they got the whole story immediately, but it is better to go back to them now before they catch him, before a trial, if you feel you didn't tell the police everything."

"This is so dumb. I didn't think the police had to know every detail. I mean, at the trial it would all be told, but the police just needed information to catch the guy. It's really dumb. I don't know if I can go back now. They know most of it, the worst part of it. . . ."

"Jennifer, can you tell me exactly what happened? It might be easier for you to talk about it now, just to go over the whole story. Can you?"

"I don't know. I think I'd rather not . . . no."

"Well . . . you should try to get the whole story out even if you don't go back to the police. Can you try to write it down? It might help you talk about it. Perhaps you could give a copy to the police to be sure they have all the details. If it goes to trial, you would have to remember all the details. It might help to get it all off your mind."

"I guess I could try to do that. I guess so."

JOURNAL - December 9, Tuesday

Will I make it till Jon gets back? Poor Jon. If I can't take care of me, how can I expect him to take care of himself PLUS me? Somehow I've got to get it all together. God, why did I mention that to Carol. I thought it would help me get my thoughts and feelings straight—to define what happened. Instead it opened Pandora's Box. It did help—I've been able to talk about details to Rosemary. But all the legal implications—does it make a difference whether it was rape or sodomy? But if it came out in a trial for the first time, it might weaken the case. I wish I'd known more about this process two months ago. It has weakened the case already whether I tell the police or not. I can hear the defense, "Now, Mrs. Barr, how could you possibly have not known you were raped till two months afterwards? Certainly everyone knows what rape is and if you were really raped you would have told the police immediately!" It is so dumb. I could never swear that I had been raped because I don't know if I was. But penetration is penetration—two inches or a half inch. I feel so stupid. It seemed I was being so careful to really get the rap on the guy. So much attention to what he looked like. Not thinking of proving a case. Of course he was guilty, we just needed to find him. There was no question about whether or not he was guilty. But was it rape? Oh, what's the difference. The psychological intent was the same, the result was the same—it has nothing to do with my vagina. And so stupid that I didn't see a doctor immediately. All this stuff about medical reports in court, they seem to be standard parts of trials. There was evidence all over me. It didn't occur to me I'd have to prove it happened! I need Jon.

I couldn't think about going back to the police. I was confused and embarrassed. I had to wait until Jon got home before I could decide, before I could move, but I did try to put it all in writing as Carol suggested. I was up until 4:30 A.M., writing my two-page description of events. Trying to remember every detail. Reliving each minute, agonizing over words to describe it. Painfully, I typed every detail in uniform black letters. The next day I edited it to leave only the cold facts unmuddled by my feelings. Now I could forget it.

Jon came home on Friday and we resumed our hibernation. I didn't call Carol back, and I didn't tell Jon the details that had concerned her. With Christmas looming before me and demanding my energy, I could not think about the matter. We fell into commercial Christmas. Jon did all the gift shopping. He wrote the cards except for those to a few close friends of mine. I wanted to write those, but as Christmas got nearer I felt more and more isolated from it. There were Christmas parties we turned down, casual friends with Christmas greetings and "Are you all set for Christmas? Bet this will be an exciting Christmas with your little ones." And I had to pull out a smile and a reply. I was beginning to hate Christmas.

JOURNAL - December 22, Monday

Wish we could have a quiet little Christmas here with just us this year. I am really dreading having to face everyone else. Jon's mother is coming tomorrow. I know I'll be so tense trying to be pleasant and failing. I wish I could hang in suspended animation and be near everyone but be ignored—no responsibilities, no obligations to talk, to be civil, to smile. I couldn't hurt anyone's feelings that way. It is really bad how crabby I am. It's not even that I say bad things accidentally. I am so cynical and pessimistic and negative and I can't help it. It used to be when I was depressed I almost enjoyed being nasty, it relieved some antagonisms I suppose. But I don't even enjoy my negativism now which is rather frightening—it's not a game, I really *feel* that way. I have *really* been so low and nervous, I hardly feel human. Wish I knew how long it would be before I feel normal again. I would never have believed such a stupid incident could shatter so much. I wish Christmas would go away.

There was no way I could avoid spending Christmas with my family. The gathering of the clan was a sacred event. I would be expected to be there, but the thought of joining a merry crowd filled me with apprehensions. I hadn't talked to them about the assault or my feelings. I didn't know how to face them because I didn't know what they were thinking. It would have been easier for me if they had brought up the topic, if they had acknowledged my trauma. I needed to know their attitude before I could expose mine. I was too aware of my vulnerability to open myself to possible criticism. The possibility of being a part of a large group pretending it was a normal Christmas was painful to think about. I would rather stay home than take the risk, but to stay home prolonged my hesitancy to face my family. Christmas was requiring too much of me. I concentrated on the part of Christmas I could handle. Nigel and Colin were oblivious to the trauma, only reacting to the glitter of the moment and they were my reason to endure Christmas.

JOURNAL - December 23, Tuesday

Flashes of the incident have been haunting me lately. I'd almost stopped thinking of it except in an uninvolved way. Last Friday night I lay awake having it all happen again. The terror, the fears have all come back to visit. I feel like I'm starting all over. I've been having horrible, gory nightmares all of a sudden. Strangely they are almost all women who are my attackers.

Jon's mother is coming tonight. I hope I can be civil.

All my energy was required to survive Christmas. We enjoyed a quiet morning with the children and in the afternoon we all tried to act normal at the family celebration. The subject was not mentioned, and the distance increased between me and those from whom I had once hoped for support.

JOURNAL - December 26, Friday

My mind is so weird. I feel like I have had such little control over it these last months. Thoughts and feelings that I don't want project themselves. I can't censure them. I've been so totally within myself—"Don't touch me"; aloof— "Don't make me react"; selfish—"Don't ask me to give or think of anyone else." I know it yet I can't change it.

How often the grotesqueness of the incident comes back

and silently takes my mind. I shake my head and say "Don't think, Jenn," but it is like telling a crazy relative to stop jibbering, "stop drooling, you're disgusting!" If I'm lucky it retreats for a while. It is so ugly. It is a leech firmly attached to my mind.

I felt a sense of achievement when the holidays were finally behind me. Jon's mother left on New Year's and I could stop pretending. I had survived the festivities.

JOURNAL - January 3, Saturday

I feel like a person again. Depression has lifted like the fog. Suddenly I look in the mirror and I am not so ugly. Having the pressures of the holidays gone has certainly done wonders. I am even motivated to do things again. I can't dream yet but I can accept the day. Things could have been a whole lot easier if we could have escaped Christmas but we made it.

CHAPTER V

A QUIETNESS came after Christmas. Finally, I was free of the festive air that had battered me with guilt and loneliness; I was free to hide or cry or frown. Finally, I could concentrate on getting myself back to normal. A few duties still had to be faced before I could completely forget the incident.

In early January, I scheduled the follow-up VD tests that Doris had urged as a precaution. Since I was referred to the Health Department by the Rape Crisis Center, they knew why I needed the tests. At the lab where I had my original tests, I had wanted to explain why I was there—*It's not what you think. . . . I had no choice. . . . I was RAPED!*—but I hid my humiliation and silently paid the five dollars.

At the Health Department I waited in a crowded room and felt very out of place. What was I doing taking advantage of free health care? I hoped I wasn't obvious.

The woman who administered the tests was older and sympathetic. I immediately felt young and sheltered.

"Have they caught the man who raped you?" For her I wanted to say yes.

While taking the smears for oral infection, she also took a throat culture for strep because I had mentioned my still-hurting throat.

"Oh, that's O.K. I could go to my doctor for that."

"Too late. I've already got it. It's simple enough to run a test on it. Ease your mind a bit more. You won't have to worry about that anyway."

When I called back later for the test results, I was embarrassed to have the secretary read that the VD was negative but there was evidence of strep.

"Should I make an appointment for you to come in and have it checked?"

"Oh . . . I . . . No . . . I'll make an appointment later." Of course I wouldn't make another appointment there. I didn't even care if I had strep.

The next step was to make an appointment with the detective to finish that story. I didn't know if it was worthwhile, but I needed to be sure everything was done. When I was ready to go back to the police, I got in touch with Carol to set up an appointment for me.

It was the middle of January before the three of us could get together. Carol stayed with me during the interview. It didn't matter except that I felt I was wasting everyone's time. I should have just kept the whole thing to myself. Why should it matter?

Jameson was still gentle and understanding. He apologized for not having made things clearer the first time and thanked me for coming back with the information.

"Rape will be added to the charges." I looked at Carol. Her expression didn't change, she wasn't surprised.

"Contact with the clitoris alone is technically rape according to the law. I don't see any problem with it. It fits your original story. You said he was masturbating; that's a general term I should have caught. You didn't say *how* he was masturbating. I can understand why it was difficult for you to give details, considering the circumstances and his other crimes against you. It is important to have all the charges on him before he is caught, so I'm glad you were able to come back in here. I know it's not easy for you." The charges weren't a decision for me to make. It was whether or not it fit the definition of the law.

I looked at the composite picture I'd done and sketched some changes in the shape of the mouth and jaw. His image had not faded in my mind.

"Since your case, there have been a number of reports of indecent exposure that sound like the same guy. Your description of the scar by his ear is our major identifying characteristic. A scar is hard to hide. Yours is the most complete identification we have on the guy. If he is still in the area, he'll probably reappear with the warm weather. This is a top-priority case here and we want to get this guy. If he's still in the area, we'll probably catch up with him . . . hopefully soon."

On the bulletin board in the hall, a copy of my composite picture took center stage. It was not crowded by notices as others were. I was surprised to see it being treated with such importance. I had stopped waiting for him to be caught but now hope was renewed. It was still possible. I hoped it was worth all the effort on everyone's part. It was hard for me to accept that other people thought the assault was so serious. These people dealt with serious crimes all the time, yet I hadn't been put in a closed file. It was surprising, but reassuring, to know others were concerned, especially those who had the power to do something if they could find him.

The addition of the rape charge left me with mixed emotions. It still didn't fit my image of rape. Rape left the victim hospitalized if not dead. It was part of the Ultimate Horror. But it was only a word. What had happened, had happened, no matter what they called it.

Fantasies of his arrest returned. How long might I wait? Should I even keep the hope that he might be caught?

JOURNAL - January 15, Thursday

Can I be sure I can identify him if he is caught? My image of him is a man under stress, with sunglasses and a hat. If I saw him relaxed without his disguise, could I be sure? So far, I am the prime witness in identifying him. I had time to study him. I look at so many men now to see if they have any similarities. It only seems to confuse me. If he is caught, I really hope I won't have any doubts. Can I really be positive about an identification? Is there really a chance he could reappear?

The thoughts of his being a warm-weather operator made me more aware of the milder days that were interrupting the bitter cold as January progressed. There were subtle signs that spring was soon coming. I felt secure on cold, rainy days. When cloudless skies allowed the temperature to rise above 40° I stayed inside.

JOURNAL - January 20, Tuesday
I wasn't alone
The trees above me, the shrubs, the weeds
In glorious autumn
Before they slept
Did they suffer the agony of human violence
Or are they immune now?
Did they expect it, accept it?
Did they cringe?
It wasn't the woods that did it.
I shouldn't fear them.
I shouldn't reject them.
They too must endure man's violence.

Though this was normally the time of year that I occupied myself with garden catalogues and dreams of daffodils, this year I closed the door to those thoughts. I picked up indoor projects that had been interrupted or postponed in the last few months. I wrote my Christmas cards with apologies. The wall that was half papered got its finishing touches. I resurrected a large needlepoint project that had been started in August for a Christmas gift for Nigel. My new goal was his birthday in March. I didn't realize the immensity of the project or the significance it would have for my survival of the year ahead. The canvas sat in the living room where it was handy to pick up when motivation or energy ebbed. It was easy to become engrossed in it. Life was returning to normal interests and routines.

I returned to the darkroom for the first time since my fateful photographic walk. The pictures I had taken that day had never been printed. Detective Jameson had asked if I had checked them for any evidence—a car or person in the background. It was worth checking, though I was usually careful about background distractions. The finished prints were very ordinary. They were not worth the printing—or the taking.

I had hesitated enrolling in another math course because I was afraid of added pressure, unsure I could face the expectations to perform. Though I had breezed through elementary math, algebra was more threatening. It was important to have Rosemary's support and she was anxious to proceed with algebra. At the last minute I chose to enroll, and the class became a helpful distraction for me. The world of math was so apart from people and emotions that when unpleasant thoughts crept up on me, my math was an escape. I could deal with numbers in a right or wrong situation.

The class was held in an old high school scheduled for remodeling. Construction had disrupted the parking lot, requiring a long walk to the building in poor lighting. The building itself was a dismal place of gray tiles and broken lockers—a 1950 edition.

On the first night of class a commotion in the room across the hall and a voice over the PA asking for anyone skilled in CPR created a tense atmosphere. Soon an ambulance arrived and a stretcher was wheeled in. No one knew what had happened. The teachers' lounge where we went for Cokes during class break was tiny, dark, and crowded. The students overflowed into the hall where we stood with our drinks as they wheeled the stretcher back through the crowd. They moved rapidly with a woman who was already hooked up to numerous tubes. Class resumed with nothing more said about it. The next week we learned that the woman had died.

JOURNAL - January 29, Thursday

I guess recovery cannot happen in a straight line. Hopefully, each time the effects of the trauma circle back they are weaker. I guess class tonight set me off. It was tense. Then Jon was really late getting home from his meeting. Nothing really to provide a reason for depression but enough to agitate my nerves. I'm probably also suffering from suppressed tension from Jon's trip last week. I'm not really depressed, but it is hard to pinpoint my feelings—uncomfortable, self-conscious, nervous. I feel like a thirteen-year-old—awkward, sensitive, too wrapped up in myself. I'm too afraid to open myself to other people's feelings and needs.

Jon was late coming home that night because he had told Pastor about our situation. Jon and I had talked about telling him, but we had been waiting. He had only been at our church for a few weeks, and I needed to know if I could trust him before he learned our secret. A part of me was relieved that he knew, a part of me was apprehensive. There was a rustling of change, but I didn't know how much or in what direction. Would he react to me differently? Would he tell anyone else? I wasn't prepared to make the first move, yet I wanted to know what would happen next. I wanted to believe he could help me resolve my feelings. He was the first person in two months to be told what had happened.

JOURNAL - February 1, Sunday

I felt so self-conscious with Pastor today. I tried to avoid him, but he said hello and I mumbled an awkward "hi" and hid my face in my hair. As I passed by him he put his hand lightly on my shoulder. He would be an easy person to lean on, but maybe he could help get me straight again too.

My hands get numb from nervousness, like I have slammed them against something. It happens at strange times when I don't even have a particular reason. I never had much patience with nervous people.

Pastor called on Monday in response to what Jon had told him.

"I can't believe this happened to you of all people."

"I don't think he was particularly choosy. He didn't much care who I was."

"I just can't understand how someone could do that to you." He was more troubled by the crime than I expected.

We arranged for him to come on Thursday afternoon, though that seemed a long way off. I wanted reassurance that I wasn't alone and I wasn't insignificant. I wanted encouragement from him to give me the strength to erase it from my mind. I wanted to give him my problems so I could forget them. But I didn't know what I would say to him. I didn't know what he expected me to say. I rehearsed different lines.

When he arrived, I was nervous and awkward. He leaned forward with his elbows on his knees, his eyes on his knuckles. There was a calmness in the quiet as he focused on his words.

"You're an amazing person, Jennifer." Instead of accepting the compliment, I put myself down with accusations of melodrama. "Jon, too. . . . He didn't give any details about it, but I assume they never caught the man?"

"No."

"And you've been carrying all this in silence for this long? . . . It's a pretty heavy load."

He didn't ask for details or suddenly probe my emotions. It was a gentle beginning that eased my fears of saying too much. He wasn't shocked or surprised by the feelings I hesitantly disclosed.

"Are you angry at God?"

"I don't know."

"How do you feel about Him?"

"I don't . . . I guess my faith isn't very strong. I haven't thought about it." It was uncomfortable to admit it to him. Normally, prayer allowed me to become detached enough from a situation to see it in a better perspective. But I couldn't pray. I couldn't even try to pray.

"He doesn't fit, does He?"

Can you really understand that feeling, man of the cloth? Can you understand that I really have no thoughts of God and accept it? Not even a conflict? He didn't push the issue further. He probed my feelings but expected no explanations. I felt that he was struggling with me to understand and I didn't feel threatened.

JOURNAL - February 5, Thursday

Talking to Pastor was so good. I think it may help. He is

coming next Thursday again "to help us grow through it." He helped focus some of my feelings. He asked if I felt anger towards the man. I struggled with the question. I felt like I should but I didn't. I couldn't even think of him as a person. That day last October when anger struck while I was driving was so overpowering. Perhaps it scared me to feel that way and I suppressed it. Now it's an unfocused anger that gives me bad feelings about people for no reason. I was taught to express my anger to a mirror and cry in my room. I was taught that it was rude to display bad feelings.

Pastor provided new questions to ponder while rocking Colin to sleep. I didn't resent the long nursing sessions at bedtime. It was very productive "think time," with a guarantee against distractions. Even my needlepoint was surrounded by lights and sounds. I struggled with the feelings Pastor had probed—guilt, anger, shame, hurt. They were all so confused.

JOURNAL - February 9, Tuesday

Listening to the news about Patti Hearst's trial, she testified that she was physically, mentally, and sexually abused and if that is true it explains the "mystery" of the good little heiress. How easily I felt devastated, destroyed, powerless. Being confused and threatened under their power, I can see how she could be "brainwashed" (as the experts like to say), to save her sanity as well as her life. In my half-hour ordeal I felt totally cut off from the "real" world, the world of reason, order, sanity. He took over my world, and to survive, I forgot there was another world. And I was only facing one man.

When Pastor came again the next Thursday, we talked about guilt feelings. I could not explain how or why I felt I was as much an accomplice to the crime as a victim. I was a necessary part of the crime; if I hadn't been there, there would have been no crime. I knew it wasn't rational but it was real.

Pastor tried to put my guilt in a different context. "If we lived in a smaller, less rigid society, do you think you might feel differently? A society where everyone knew you, and justice could be dealt out freely. . . ."

It was a puzzling supposition, but I thought about our system, of the crime being "against the State," of my being the "State's witness," of my testimony being judged. My vision of the witness box became one of a scaffold holding the assailant and me side by side. I didn't like the thoughts that Pastor's questions had provoked. My logical mind refused to admit guilt, but logic had lost its edge. I tried to walk away from the image I didn't want to see, but instead I crashed into it. A door slammed shut as I withdrew within myself. I sat clutching my knees, trying to escape to the trees behind and above Pastor's head.

"It is so hopeless. Nothing matters. I don't want to do anything. I've tried to get into my old interests, but they don't matter anymore."

Pastor was upset by my distance but could not coax me back. As he stood to leave he put his hand on my head. It was a sincere gesture, but I nearly exploded in panic. It reminded me that, though I fought to escape, I was still locked in my frozen body. I couldn't speak. I was caught between two worlds.

I couldn't push the depression back into its box after

Pastor left. I had been telling myself that everything was O.K., that it was time for full recovery and I wouldn't allow myself to waste anymore of my life on the issue. Things were getting better. Everything had been done to finish the story. I didn't think about whether or not he'd be caught—I'd deal with that if it happened. I had been getting back into normal routines, successfully burying my emotions. But the box was sprung open and it was filled with despair. I could not face my feelings and went back to my needlepoint.

JOURNAL - February 13, Friday

I am so sick of being a "rape victim." I want to be me again. No one is making me be a rape victim. Jennifer Barr is always so busy, has lists of things she wants to do, but I don't want to do anything now. I only do what is required. I can't even write lists because nothing is important, nothing is interesting. My normal depression cures don't seem to work. Even thinking of the cabin at the lake doesn't excite me. I don't feel depressed, just tired of it all. Maybe I'm so used to being depressed I don't even feel it anymore.

JOURNAL - February 14, Saturday

Had such a grim dream this morning. It was very confused. On a campus, I had one friend and we were both cripples and I didn't have underpants on. I felt helpless and different, I was physically deformed and an object of ridicule. A second dream was an assault dream. I encountered the man who attacked me in October and he recognized me. He grabbed me and tore off my blouse. Though he threatened me, he let me go. I was afraid to tell the police and

was tossing in turmoil when Jon suddenly shook me awake.
He was impatient with the kids and wanted help. What a
horrible way to begin the day.

Rosemary listened to my description of my dreams and
nodded. She recognized my fear of having people dislike
me. Even in the second dream I didn't want the assailant to
hate me. We couldn't think of a logical reason for wanting
to be prom queen, but we both wanted people to smile at us.
I was afraid people would think of me as different. A stereotype of a rape victim could become a judgment of me. My
defenses were still too fragile to face public opinion.

JOURNAL - February 17, Tuesday
Wish I could understand what sets off my strange moods.
Last night at a church meeting I was so withdrawn. It had
been a normally exhausting day and everyone was friendly,
but I wanted to hide. I wanted to just listen and crawl out
only if I wanted to say something. I was trembling by the
meeting's end and I couldn't even say why. I wish the people at church knew, but how can I tell it at this point, almost three months later?

Warm weather came in February. It was a year that I
didn't welcome an early spring. I didn't open the windows
to invite fresh breezes. When Nigel pleaded to play outside,
I stood by my window to see that he didn't leave the patio. I
didn't encourage his budding independence. I was afraid to
have him out of my sight. My dreams of discovering birds'
nests and watching caterpillars with my son were buried
deep. I didn't want to cry over what could not be, but I was

dreading spring. I was dreading being torn between my love of nature and my fear of it. It was hard to think that it could be a long time before I could enjoy moments of solitude outside again. All that had been precious was no longer beautiful. Silence was isolation, sunshine exposed vulnerability, a fluttering bird created tensions. When I stepped outside, my eyes darted to observe any movement, any suspicious object, any lurking strangers. The trees provided no gentleness.

Though I still struggled to cover my ugly scars, at night they were exposed. I was terrorized by nightmares of being chased. I would wake up in total panic when I became trapped. I had to waken Jon to comfort me, and then I felt guilty for disturbing him.

In the middle of February, my nightmares suddenly stopped and were replaced by curious dreams about houses. There were three dreams in one week about modern houses that were closed in: One was underground, another had no doors to the lush forest just outside the glass walls. Each house had evidence of strange people in it, innocent intruders but always unseen. Though each house was different, each dream was very similar. Did they just reflect my seclusion and desire to be outside? And the strangers passing through or living in dark chambers of my houses . . . who were they?

JOURNAL - February 18, Wednesday

I still feel insignificant. When people turn to listen to me, I freeze. Don't listen to me! Why should anyone care what I have to say? It is almost like they are intruding even though I am speaking. I feel embarrassed when someone listens or looks at me or is nice to me. I get upset so easily. I do feel shame, though there is no rational reason for it and I don't understand its source. Is it shame that I was weak and didn't fight back? No, I think I handled it as well as I could. In the supposed rape fantasies, a woman is supposed to enjoy it. Am I lacking something that I didn't enjoy an iota of it, that I never had a rape fantasy? Somehow my shame is connected with the gentler side of the assailant, and with his attempts to turn me on. If he had been just violent to me, it would have been easier. But he made me feel sympathy for him and guilty that I didn't enjoy it like he wanted me to. Society's attitudes about women and sex have been so unreal, it isn't surprising that I have screwed-up feelings about it.

I was beginning to sort out feelings. In my quiet moments I isolated particular feelings and examined them one by one. Sex with Jon was still tense. I avoided it whenever possible. It brought on flashbacks and as the cycle built, Jon pressured me more. I felt guilty until I felt I had no choice and succumbed. I had no power against my guilt, and felt powerless, helpless, used, raped. My anger was veiled in shame that I was a woman. If I were not guilty of being a woman, life would be so much easier. But the seed of recognition and its resolution were a long way apart. I had many feelings to sort out and deal with at the same time, and Jon patiently waited for me to smile at him.

JOURNAL - February 23, Monday

I wonder if I'll ever unwitch or if I've had a permanent personality change. I find myself constantly fidgeting whenever I am with people. Perhaps there is hope if I can learn to enjoy people again. I tolerate people more now, but I still want to be left alone. Don't look at me, don't talk to me, don't listen to me, and especially don't get close to me, emotionally or physically. I still feel the shell that sets me apart. If someone touches me, it's like an electric shock. If I feel someone is probing my emotions I shrink into a corner. So reserved, so distant. If I can sit and watch and listen, I can begin to relate to other people but it is lost when they become aware of me, when I am made vulnerable. When I was a shy teenager, I felt a lot like I do now and I got over it then. I convinced myself there was nothing to fear, I was just like everyone else. I'm not sure that is the right alley now, I'm not like everyone else. I know my vulnerability. I've lost the faith that brought me out of teenage shyness— the faith in the ideals of beauty and goodness. That is my basic struggle now—to build a new foundation to have faith in. I'm not sure that it is people, God, ideals, me. . . . The old rocks don't seem so stable anymore. I do have faith in Jon, in his goodness, in his companionship. That is my faith these days, which makes me depend on the poor man so much. Right now it is hard to think of anything else I have faith in. Tomorrow I should sit down and make a list of things to believe in. It's late now.

JOURNAL - February 26, Thursday

I saw Pastor today. I felt defenses beginning to crack. There were things I wanted to say. I was fighting tears but couldn't explain them to him. I was in my shell and he was trying so desperately to draw me out. I realized while we were talking that I don't want to be the "old Jennifer Barr," but I couldn't say it. I don't like her. I am beginning to see a lot in her that I wasn't aware of. How can I get rid of her? Who would I be if I did?

Part of the fear of telling people about what happened seems to be that I'm afraid of not being believed. It is silly. I don't remember anyone ever not believing me about anything. Why should it even matter if people believe me or not?

A new series of rap sessions was scheduled to begin on February 28. Though I had missed the support and opportunity to talk to other victims during the two months between sessions, Jon questioned whether I should attend because it had been so physically and emotionally draining. Though my body did react strongly, it was a necessary extraction. There was so much I needed to learn and understand that I felt my survival depended on it.

The rap group met in a private home rather than the sterile, empty office building and was made up of the same people as the first group. It was immediately more comfortable. I needed the reassurance from other victims, who could share the thoughts, fears, and frustrations I felt. They made my feelings more understandable, and I didn't have to give reasons for my feelings for them to understand. For two hours of the week I didn't feel alone and different.

I began to talk more openly in the group. If they could share their weakness, I could share mine. My latent trust was nourished and grew each week. Even Leila, who seemed to have reached some higher plane of living, had fears and insecurities. We talked about current problems, our progress and regressions, new obstacles, and how we handled the old ones. I felt a warmth and kinship with these women.

One Sunday in late February, my progress with my fears was jolted by words in a sermon I wasn't ready to hear. "We try to hide in cocoons but God sees through them. He sees us squirming inside. . . ." I couldn't face the thought that my shell might not be invincible. I felt totally exposed. I felt the spotlight scanning the congregation, landing on me; the scarlet letter burning on my breast. There was no place to hide.

I tried to explain to Jon afterwards why I was upset.

"But God isn't a *person!* I don't see how you can lump Him together with your other fears. Why are you afraid of Him?"

"Him, Jon! That's just it. He! He! He! *He,* the Father. *He,* the Son. Even *He,* the Holy Spirit. Why is it *He* always! A special pronoun would be better. Beauty, Goodness, and Mercy are feminine traits anyway. Why not She? Even sometimes . . . or one of the Three. *He* can't understand how I feel. I don't want anything to do with Him who can enter my mind and body at will! How could you understand anyway!" I snapped, angry at Jon for not understanding, angry at Jon for being a man.

JOURNAL - February 29, Sunday

I feel so uncomfortable in church. I feel guilty when I retreat from people there. One woman came up to me after church, "What's the matter, Jennifer? You look so sad today." I mumbled something about colds and such. I wanted to thank her for her concern. I wanted to be honest with her, but I didn't dare. I'm in such a dark tunnel. I feel like I'm not very sane at times. I feel like I'm being melo-dramatic still. How can it still be affecting me so much? I function fine in situations where I willingly leave my shell behind, when I feel confident or when I am confident that my shell will protect me from unwanted or feared inti-macies. But at church my shell cracks and I feel defenseless. Somehow I should let it out soon. Hiding something causes guilt feelings or is it hidden because of guilt feelings? I wish I could also stop feeling such fears. I am so aware of how vulnerable I am and it hits me with such panic when I real-ize there is no one around for help or there is no escape.

That Sunday afternoon there was a planning meeting for the church garden. I had worked on it and believed in it in previous years and I wanted to see that it continued. It was a beautiful day and we stood talking in the parking lot as everyone arrived. As they talked and I listened, there was a series of gunshots in the woods behind the church. I froze. The men turned their heads and wondered aloud as we went inside for the meeting. I wanted to ask someone to in-vestigate the shots, to call the police. We couldn't ignore it. Flashbacks of my unheard screams filled my head. I couldn't speak. Through the window I watched a police car drive into the parking lot, investigating a car parked by the woods.

"Hey, Joe, they're after you. Isn't that your car?"

"Yeah. Wonder what he thinks he's doing?"

"I don't know, but at least it's keeping him off the streets, catching speeders."

While everyone laughed, I wanted to scream. I wanted

to run out to the car to explain to the officer. I steeled my nerves.

"Well you should tell him, Joe." My controlled words weren't heard in the laughter.

"He's even taking down your license number. Hope you don't have anything bad on your record."

He's investigating the shooting, you oafs!! Don't you guys realize someone could be dead out there, and you're letting him waste his time while you laugh!

My head was screaming, but I couldn't bring the words out. I went to the ladies' room to calm down or vomit. I was afraid that if I released those fears and frustrations, more than I wanted might slip out.

JOURNAL - March 1, Monday

The discussion at rap session last Saturday again brought back my experience with Dan when I was in college. It is unbelievable now how totally guilty I felt and suppressed it. I had never told anyone about it. I couldn't even think about it. I mentioned it quietly to the group this time, "a situation that got out of my control." When I got home the memories began to gnaw at me, to slip out of the guilt bag enough to see it wasn't my fault. It didn't fit the "classic portrayal" of rape. If he were a rapist, he would have attacked me the first time I went out with him but he never even held my hand. I asked for it, after all I went into his apartment willingly. He didn't have a weapon. I had been warned to stay away from him. I should have known. But the shame. Hiding the bruises. Worried about the bleeding but not even considering a doctor. I was so scared, I didn't feel like I had a choice. I'd never been "roughed up" before.

I was petrified when he pushed me down. I knew he was going to have his way one way or another, so I didn't fight him. And the fears of seeing him on the street. His insults about it were so horribly cruel. And his calls afterward, more insults about why I didn't want to go out for a beer with him. And I just made feeble excuses. Oh, it makes me so angry now! I feel angrier about that right now than the recent incident. At least this time it was clear-cut. It's easier to say "but there was a knife at my throat." I have been carrying such stupid guilt for so long!

One evening, soon after the experience with Dan was brought to mind, I began to talk to Jon about experiences I had had with men. The discussion began on dating relationships in general, but when he was receptive I was propelled into specifics I had never shared with him. I jumped from tale to tale throughout my adolescence. "And then there was the guy who wanted to set me up as a prostitute," I told him. I told him all the things I'd felt guilty about. I'd felt it was something about me, something I did or was bad. I was never taught how to handle a bad situation—just "be careful," "be a good girl." Even as I told the tales, I could see a pattern of similar situations and guilt building up. We laughed about them. Some were so ridiculous—the dinner party where a married man was all over me while his wife announced her first pregnancy. He would not keep his hands off me for a minute and didn't seem a bit concerned who saw it. I was so embarrassed that I left the party early.

Jon was on his feet, the devil in his eyes. "You should have said for everyone to hear 'If you have to act like an animal, go find a bitch that's in heat!'"

I loved it. It had never occurred to me to put a man on the defensive. The thought of embarrassing someone else was unheard of! Since I'd never shared these awkward moments with anyone, I had had no perspective on them. They all seemed so different after I told Jon and he didn't think I was horrible. He couldn't understand how I could possibly have felt guilty.

As I was shedding the accumulated self-condemnation that had always been a barrier in relationships with me, my faith and trust in Jon grew. I was making progress with some of my conflicts, but I was also acutely aware of the problems I still had to overcome. The road was slow, and when I paused to look ahead, the winding road seemed to lead endlessly through barren wastelands.

JOURNAL - March 3, Wednesday

He counted to fifty as I went under the porch. He'd never find me there, no one could see me from outside. "Ready or not, here I come." I crouched and held my breath. I could see Him wander looking, walking. Behind the tree, inside the bush. It was really dark inside. He called my name but I kept still. A spider dropped on my hand. I froze and stared but dared not jump. Slowly, so controlled, I brushed him off. It was only little. I wasn't afraid. But I twitched at the thought of the unknown others hiding there. I looked out again but He had gone. I thought I heard Him around the house. I waited and listened, yes still there. Some giggles before the silence, from out on the street I thought. Was it Him? and who else? Were they laughing at me? Did He leave to go home? I started to peek but heard them again. He said He was looking for me. "She'll come out when she's tired of playing the game. Let's go sit under the tree." They sat and they giggled. I watched it all. They wouldn't catch me with their trick. Did He think I'd forget and come out after all. It was a long while before they got up. He called me once more, the last time He said. Then there was silence again. Had He given up and gone away, I was afraid of another trick. I knew He'd never find me there. Never, yet I waited still more. Never, and I waited still. Never, and I waited. Never.

Jon saw what I had written. It upset him.
"Who are you hiding from?"
"I don't know. Whatever is threatening me."
"It's really grim. Why did you write it?"
"Is it so grim?"

JOURNAL - March 5, Friday

I can't imagine how I'd survive this if I didn't have Jon and the kids. They are all I have interest in, all I enjoy these days. I feel like I'm starting all over with the depression. I'm back in December again except that I have less excuse for it now, less confidence in time. I have made some progress. I'm not back in December but I feel so totally empty. Before I was waiting for the "old me" to return but now evaluating the "old me" I don't want that. I want the enthusiasm, the motivation but somehow I need to find a more complete me, a "real me." Not one haunted by guilt, pretending to be strong. I did a lot of pretending without realizing it. How does one start from scratch after thirty years? How do I "create" a better me? What is there of value? What do I latch on to as a beginning? I have Jon and the kids; there must be a beginning there. But what? I only want to sit and cling to what I have. Even my plants are all dying.

I wasn't handling my feelings the way I had expected I could. I had run out of obstacles to blame. There was no external pressure that I had to fight off. I had the time needed for healing, but my fears weren't disappearing. My shell against the world hardened and allowed no emotions to permeate it. I was too deep in the mire to pull myself out, and I was scared. Margot, the social worker Doris had recommended, had been mentioned at rap sessions too as someone sensitive to rape victims. I decided to trust the recommendations and called her.

"Yes. I can see you next Thursday at nine. O.K.?"

"O.K." but the tightness in my voice must have let out. *Can I hold on for a whole week more?*

"I could squeeze you in at eleven tomorrow if next week is too far away."

"Yes, yes, thank you." I didn't want to sink any deeper.

Margot was an attractive young woman who smiled cheerfully instead of giving the silent stares over glasses that I had imagined. She listened, reacted, and asked. I didn't feel scrutinized. I sketched for her what had happened and how my shell was constructed. The hour passed very quickly; we had hardly more than introduced ourselves. She made arrangements for me to see her again on Monday morning.

I wasn't sure I could face rap session on Saturday. I had been doing so much better than during the last series and I didn't want to disclose my new depression. But I was afraid of their questions if I didn't go. It would be easier to go and just keep quiet. There was a new member there that day who drew attention away from my tenseness. No one probed into the quietness I was able to maintain.

Jon was away that day, so when I came home I tried to nap when the kids napped. I was beginning to relax when I heard a noise, a small noise as of something falling. A toy from a crib? A clumsy footstep? What type of noise it was faded as my imagination changed the sound to match the possibilities racing through my head. My heart was pounding, my hands clammy. Hearing no more noises, I breathed deeply till the paralyzing panic passed and I went into the kitchen. The house was still. As I stood at the counter with dishrag in hand, tears suddenly streamed down my face as reality began slipping past me. My body was trembling to be released from my frozen posture. Thoughts of the kids gave me the power to reach the phone. Someone had to help, someone had to be with the kids. I called Karen from the rap group. She came without hesitation.

"Jennifer, if you really flipped out, you wouldn't have been able to call me, would you? You called and you asked for help and that's O.K. That's what we're all for. It's hard on you and it's frightening, but you're getting through it. I'll stay till Jon comes home so you won't have to be alone anymore today if you'd like. Being alone when you're scared is rough, but you're really handling this fine. Really you are. You called me, Jennifer, and everything is O.K. now. Right? It's O.K. You haven't flipped out. You're doing fine."

Even if I didn't believe her, it felt good to hear her encouragement. She made sense and she stayed with me until my imagination was exhausted and the room was quiet again.

JOURNAL - March 7, Sunday

I'm worse than ever now about being alone. I'd really felt rather safe at home with the doors locked. Now I jump at every noise. Perhaps it is the warm weather, with having doors and windows open more often. Perhaps just feeling unsure everything is locked. There are more people and noises outside now, too much to check on. Jon said he'd allow a dog now. I hope he means it, that he wouldn't regret it if I got one. I think it would help me feel safer. It would be a good distraction anyway—something to demand my attention.

When I saw Margot on Monday, she focused on specific feelings. I was very tense, afraid of what I might say, afraid I might learn she couldn't help. I still didn't know what I could expect from her. I didn't know where this venture would turn me.

"You know you have used the word 'trapped' four times in the last few minutes." Trapped, yes. I did feel I was trapped. I'd turned back on my walk to avoid the man on the bridge and walked into a worse situation. Why didn't the man hear my screams? Or was it the same man? Where had everyone else gone? Had they left conveniently? Had they heard my screams and reacted to them as we had reacted to the shots at the church last Sunday? Maybe no one heard, maybe I was really alone at the one moment in my life when I didn't want to be far from civilization.

Even nature had betrayed me. Nature in her beauty was a part of it all. It had lured me to those woods and did not lose its beauty after witnessing the ugliness. In a movie the wind would come with ominous clouds, but beauty stood there in mocking immunity. I had gone to nature for peace. It made me whole. It made the world sane. How could it betray my trust? How could I have lain there amid all its beauty and been tortured by hatred, violence, ugliness? How could nature have been so cruel?

I was too exhausted to be alone with my thoughts after I saw Margot and spent the rest of the day with Rosemary. In my depression I had been avoiding Rosemary. I was afraid she would lose patience with me, but she was still there ready to listen and talk. She wanted to know about Margot and encouraged me to trust her.

"Did you hear about those people murdered downtown?" She changed the topic when the discussion of my morning waned.

"No, you know I can't watch the news and that's precisely why."

"But, Jennifer, this was so horrible. I just can't stand it. I'm so upset about it, so you'll just have to listen to me for a change. I just can't understand. Six people all together in one room. Six *men* in one room shot, one by one, by one man with a shotgun! A shotgun that had to be reloaded!" Her voice rose, her face was flushed. "Here. It's in the paper. You have to read it."

I struggled with her to understand how it could have happened. With six men against one gun, it seemed someone should have been able to do something. Did they just not believe that it was happening? Did they each wait for someone else to make a move rather than take the risk themselves? Were they totally paralyzed by fear? It was like the eight nurses murdered in Chicago, but this time it was men and the murders occurred right in front of their eyes. We tried to envision it. I knew how paralyzing fear could be. I

knew how hard a mind would fight to change an irrational situation into something comprehensible. "He only wants our money. He wouldn't possibly kill us if we gave it to him." In our shock, we hypothesized what the victims might have been able to do to save their lives. It pushed me to think what I could have done, should have done.

JOURNAL - March 8, Monday

People feel so impotent so easily—even facing death. It is important to think about fighting back. Today I could even picture myself fighting for my life. I'd never really fantasized a situation where I would physically fight. Men are better trained to think that way. I feel so good to have even imagined how I might fight. It would be good to know what my strengths are, what my limitations are, what it feels like to hit someone. Tonight I had a fantasy about how I might have escaped last fall. I had gone over it all so many times and it seemed like I had done my best but that was what trapped me so. He could have killed me! To what point would I have remained passive, believing I wouldn't be hurt if I stayed calm and followed his orders? What hope was there that it couldn't happen again exactly the same way? With the knife at my throat or ribs I was powerless, but there were moments later when he was off guard. I had no clothes, so it would have been humiliating to run for help but could I have run naked if my life depended on it? I might have been able to grab his shirt from the ground for some covering. I still would have been terrorized and humiliated by it but I would not have been defeated, not rendered powerless. Whether it would have been wise or better than what I did is not important. What is important is that I

can see an alternative—even if it is only a fantasy and five
months late! There is hope though. Hope that I can depend
on me when I know now that I can't depend on others who
can't or won't help. It is such a revolutionary thought! I feel
so good. There is hope that I don't need to be intimidated
by any situation. I know that other people have weaknesses,
they are intimidated too, afraid to stick their necks out and
it has finally gotten through my head that not all people are
worth thinking about as people. If a man means to murder,
it is no time to think of his feelings. In so many situations
we sit back, thinking someone else will do something. In an
emergency *I* must act and not wait for someone else to do
something. The shooting in the woods last Sunday, *I* should
have called the police. It might have been innocent but
no one should have been shooting. I am so full of self-
confidence right now. I am still nervous and I haven't tested
my confidence outside the house yet. I'm sure it will get battered and tremble but there is such HOPE about it all.
There is so much to settle yet but I've broken the bonds that
were enslaving me.

CHAPTER VI

We sailed into the lagoon at midday for a picnic among the water lilies.

"Do you see the fish down there? They glow in the dark, in the shadows under the lilies. Here, I'll catch you some." Pete dipped his net into the water to bring up a few twitching minnows with luminous stripes. They seemed grateful when he released them back into the darkness of the water.

"Why would a fish want to glow so that all its predators could see it even in the dark?"

"Haven't figured that out yet. I've only been watching them about a week. I haven't found much information on them. I might be forced to go into the city unless I can find someone else to retrieve some books for me." The city meant cars and people, traffic signals, and No Dogs Allowed signs. Pete preferred his woods and water, with enough money to maintain his boat and enough time to explore.

Our sail with Pete that March day was my first venture into nature again. Since we hadn't seen our hermit friend since before Colin's birth, Jon was anxious to accept his invitation and my mother agreed to baby-sit all day. I knew it wouldn't be like the old days. I had discussed the trip in detail with Margot and she had urged me to go, but I wasn't sure I was ready to test my nerves so dramatically. I was uncertain how I would react to being on a boat with no place to hide, no place to run. What if my confidence didn't hold? What if we were miles from shore and I exploded? How would Pete react? What if I ruined everyone's day? I cautiously decided to take the risk.

That day Jon understood I was planning to take it one step at a time. He understood that he would do the explaining if we had to change plans. As we walked through the woods he held my hand and we followed close to Pete. "This isn't too bad," I thought. "I don't feel panicky with them." It was such a remote area it was hard to imagine any intruders, and the woods were not closed in with spring foliage yet.

As the day progressed and I still felt calm, I even tried to force unsettling thoughts into my head. "What if—" My jaw would set in anger but no sweaty palms, no shaking, no retreating from the thoughts. I wasn't trusting fate or people or nature yet, but I discovered that the terrifying fears of being helpless did not disrupt the day. I was satisfied with my day and slept on the drive home.

JOURNAL - March 22, Monday

I had another house dream and finally they make sense. It was our house but I discovered a huge new part of it. It was beautiful—a huge Victorian room, filled with exciting discoveries, stained glass windows, ornate beds, a fantastic player piano with inlaid wood that played violin music. I was so excited I ran to have everyone come and see it too. *The house was me!* The excitement of discovering a whole new part of me, filled with things I've wanted and more. The old-house dreams, with the unknown people and hidden places, were me when I was trying to get hold of myself, feeling that there was a part of me that I didn't know. They make such sense now.

I was feeling exuberantly confident. After months of confinement I was ready to run through the fields, yelling, "I'm me! I can do things. I'm just like anyone else and I'm not afraid!" I felt good talking to people. I stopped shrugging my shoulders apologetically whenever I talked. Words came clearly and well ordered. And I could listen and hear again.

At the next rap session, I talked to those who were counselors with the Rape Crisis Center about becoming a Rape Crisis counselor. I was anxious to do something with my new energy. I wanted to comfort other victims and give them the hope I had finally found. I wanted to put all my ideas and thoughts into action. The next training program for counselors was scheduled for May.

With my new confidence I canceled my appointments with Margot.

Jon learned that he had to make another trip to California in April and this time I was ready to go with him. He could only take a week of vacation, so we had to choose which of our favorite places we would visit. Yosemite, Point Lobos, Mendocino, Death Valley all beckoned us and we spent many hours over the map of possibilities. Vacation dreams were half the excitement of travel.

The last Sunday of March provided a test of my new assertiveness. My mother invited us for dinner for a family gathering. It was important to her that we attend for a complete reunion, but Jon was overburdened with work and time was precious to him. I was the compromisor. Jon agreed to a limited visit. I explained the situation to Mom and said, "We'll come about four but we absolutely must leave by seven."

"O.K. I'll plan dinner for four-thirty. You haven't seen your sister in so long, you know. I know she's anxious to see you. But I know you're busy."

We arrived to find my sister's plans had been changed and she wouldn't arrive till five. It was closer to six when she came. We sat down to eat at 7:04. Jon was pacing. I was fuming. I felt our needs didn't matter as much as my sister's. Her excuse for being late was that she stopped to visit someone on the way. I had put out so much effort and no one could understand why I was impatient. I was furious at everyone. Perhaps the situation hadn't been explained to my sister, but no one even offered us an apology. The careful planning with my mother could have been with a brick wall. Didn't she hear me? Didn't she believe me? And Jon had trusted my planning, so his aggravation was dumped on me.

JOURNAL - March 29, Monday

I feel so frustrated with everyone. So much empty chitchat,

denying feelings, denying basic human needs. I resent the power of men, the self-demeaning attitudes of women. I haven't even been around men who flaunt their power. I resent Jon's power. People listen to him, expect things from him. Last night we talked and he said how being a house-wife limited my exposure, that's why people didn't listen to me. He was trying to be helpful, trying to help me analyze the situation but I exploded. Jon is a scientist. Certainly in his field he has superior knowledge but on every other topic I have the advantage. I am freer to spend time thinking of policies, politics, philosophy. Why are his opinions more im-portant than mine! And the weekend event! Why do I have to apologize when I arrange plans. I never argue with his plans. I treat evenings and weekends as his time. My time is more flexible. I can do "my thing" during his work hours— sometimes!! It is reasonable to try to do my things that way but when occasionally I make a weekend or evening plan, he should be as willing to go along with it as I am with his plans. It's not his fault, it's my fault, it's society's fault. Women's thoughts, plans, desires are fine as long as they don't interfere with a man's.

That week my exuberance ebbed as my frustrations mounted, but the frustrations took a new form. They were external frustrations. Once I finally was able to look in the mirror and see a real person behind my features, I expected everyone else to see it too.

JOURNAL - March 30, Tuesday

I'm feeling unsettled again. I lie awake at night and the gro-tesqueness returns. I don't feel fear, I feel bitter. I feel let down. My determination can't face reality. "I will not be intimidated," yet I am. "I won't let other people's hang-ups get me down," yet I do.

That night, lying awake amid ugly thoughts, flashbacks of his penis in my mouth pounded in my head. I gnashed my teeth till they ached. *Why didn't I bite the hell out of him? I could have taken my souvenir to the police so they could just match parts. How dare anyone treat me like that? How dare anyone treat* anyone *like that?* I thrashed and I clutched the bedding. My body ached to smash things, the mirror, the windows, anything big that could shatter. I turned on the lights and got up. The rage didn't disappear with the darkness. I paced the kitchen and the living room, trying to hold my shaking body from violence. All I knew was rage. I took a tranquilizer left from October. I wanted to scream till there was no scream left. I was exploding with the anger that had been buried for five months. I did not know what anger was until that night.

The next day I called Margot's office for an appointment. They scheduled one for April 15—more than two weeks away. I called back to ask for Margot to call me. Maybe she could help me by phone to hold me until I could see her. When she called, she said she could fit me in the next day. I wondered whose time I was horning in on.

When I saw Margot the next morning, I was frightened by the anger that hadn't lost any intensity. I'd never experienced such violent anger and I didn't know how to contain it. I told Margot how my anger had been set off, how intensely it had surfaced, and how obsessed I was by it. Margot responded with stronger than usual words.

"You're so hard on yourself. You want to take care of

everything by yourself, but sometimes others could help you. If you could open up and talk more . . . Anger isn't a horrible sin. People would understand and you could find relief in just letting off steam. People may even be relieved to hear that you're angry. You expect so much of yourself. Is control really so important for you? What do you think would happen if you lost control, totally let go?"

"I'd probably scream and cry until someone carted me away and I could spend my life staring into space."

"Do you think it would be that easy?"

"No, they'd probably try to cure me."

"If you could learn to let go, that might be the cure you need—if you could learn to express your feelings rather than hide them. Learn to explode. You need to see that losing control isn't the end of the world. If you feel like smashing things, find something you can smash that you won't feel guilty about afterwards. Smash your garbage, smash old bottles, tear up old magazines. The world won't stop if you go ahead and have a temper tantrum."

"I don't know if I can. I'd feel so dumb. . . . I don't think it would work. I get so angry I can't think. I'd hurt something I shouldn't. . . ."

"But you have to let it out somehow. What is it that makes you feel so mad? What sets off your anger?"

"Him. I just see his . . . penis . . . and his big belly. He made me . . . I just can't stand it!" My fingernails stabbed my palms as I clutched my anger in my hands.

"What would you like to do to him if he were here now?"

"If he were here? If he were . . ." I took a deep breath. "I'd like to . . . cut . . . him. I'd like to wave the knife

under his nose and slowly cut off . . . no, just mutilate him
. . . just leave his penis dangling. How could he have *done*
that? Why *me?* Oh, I want to tear him to shreds. I want him
to know what he has done to me and my family. I want him
to *burn* for the suffering he brought!" My hands were numb
and my cheeks burned like red-hot iron.

"You have to let it out, Jennifer. Somehow you have to
tell people your anger. If you can't talk to people about it,
write about it. I know you write in your journal, but that is
still just keeping it to yourself. Let your anger out. Write to
the newspaper, write to your congressman, write an article.
But don't try to hold it all inside you."

"Yeah, I could get everyone else mad and they could go
around smashing things. That wouldn't be nice." I was hesi-
tant to agree with Margot, but I had already found it helpful to write angry letters about things that had bothered me
for years but were suddenly unbearable. With Margot's encouragement, perhaps I might even mail some. At the worst,
someone at a faraway desk would think I was irrational. I decided to go home and slap stamps on some envelopes and
look for things I could legitimately complain about.

JOURNAL - April 1, Thursday

I really needed to talk to Margot to tell someone about what
specifically set off my anger. The initial act of putting his
penis in my mouth and telling me to suck it is really the
hardest flashback to deal with, the hardest thing to talk
about. Why does it make me so angry? Why was it worse
than anything else that day? After that I was numbed to
whatever else happened. It was the shock, the repulsion,
and I had no choice. Being forced to take off my clothes

doesn't come back to me and bring such anger. Perhaps it was that I expected that he would do things to me but not that I would have to do anything. The passive parts are easier to accept. That *I* did something was so much a part of the guilt. "He did this and he did that" is easy to say compared to saying "I sucked his penis." I still cringe. I couldn't have done that. Yet I did. That he had such power to force me to do it makes me violently angry. What was the limit of what he could have forced me to do? How could anyone hold such power over me?!

I had regular weekly appointments with Margot for the next two months. I needed her to keep my balance. She helped me understand the emotions that were finally surfacing with such force. She was the voice of common sense when I couldn't find mine.

JOURNAL - April 4, Sunday
Had such a frustrating dream Saturday night, a rape dream. I was raped by a friend's boyfriend. I didn't feel terror as in previous rape dreams, I felt hatred. The friend and Nigel walked in right afterwards and the friend was mad that I'd taken her lover and Nigel came to me innocently. "What's the matter, Mama?"

When I learned the date of the Rape Crisis Center training, I ached with frustration. It was scheduled for May 1, when we were planning to be in California. I wanted so much to do both and neither could be rescheduled. It seemed so unfair. There would be another training session in August, so I'd have to wait till then. Perhaps I wasn't as ready as I had thought to face another victim anyway.

JOURNAL - April 7, Wednesday

Things seem so frustrating these days. Even seeing Margot seems unproductive. I felt like I was just "checking in" with her today. Nothing really to say. Why should I worry if I failed Floor Scrubbing 101? I just get so sick of the chaos here. Is it possible to have control even over one's house?

I was easily frustrated and often in tears, but my children were often the source of encouragement.

"Mama, while I was drinking my bottle I heard you were crying. Are you O.K. now, Mama?"

"Yes, Nigel. I'm better now. I was just upset and cried a little but I'm O.K. now."

"What made you O.K.? Did Papa make you feel better?"

"Yes, you beautiful son, Papa listened and that helped. Do you want me to get you another bottle?"

"No, I want Papa to get me a bottle and you give me a kiss."

How could I feel totally unappreciated. There were some rewards in my life, some recognition.

JOURNAL - April 12, Monday

Wish I knew why I feel so down. I'm so crabby I just feel like kicking things. Looking for something to be mad at. I tried throwing things like Margot suggested but it didn't seem to help. I felt silly. I couldn't make it be my anger. Writing angry letters helps more. I haven't mailed any but it helps to write them. Maybe I should mail some.

I just mopped the kitchen floor. That helped get rid of some frustrations. Wish I could define my feelings. I think I want to be listened to more.

My relationship with Jon was threatened by my emotional upheavals. On my last night of class before our California trip, Jon called to say he had to work late. When I couldn't find a sitter, he said matter-of-factly I'd have to miss math class. I was furious. He took it for granted that his work was more important than my class. His work obviously was important and he had to do it, but I also had to go to class. I'd miss two classes the next week anyway. But the anger came because he didn't just say "We have a problem of conflicting important things." He said what he was doing was more important than what I was doing. We finally found a sitter to resolve the issue. Even though I realized the situation was not Jon's fault, I was so angry I was ready to take the kids down to his office on my way to class.

When I saw Margot the next day, I was confused by my unpredictable emotions. "Why am I acting like this?" She probed until I saw how things were related. Now that I was feeling like a human again, I was angry about being treated so inhumanely and was determined never to let it happen again. People must respect me as a person, must treat me as valuable. I was taking any slight as a sign people were treating my concerns as trivial.

JOURNAL - April 23, Friday

I wonder who I'll be when I get out of all this. Somehow I must become more open and more receptive. People have always described me as sophisticated, aloof, snobbish, reserved or cold, depending on how well they tolerated it. I love warm people and I really want to be more open. It should be so much easier in dealing with people.

On April 25 we left for California. Our flight there was disastrous. We had to change planes in Chicago, which was having a late spring snow. Since no planes could land there, we were taken to another airport and told to stay on board because the weather could clear anytime for take-off. The airlines personnel met my anger and frustrations with coldness. Despite the thirteen hours of confinement with no food, the kids were more patient and cooperative than I was! I expressed my frustration strongly to the airline employees in spite of the futility of my efforts. My assertiveness surprised me and it kept my anger from backfiring into a depression at the end of the flight.

On the first day of our stay, Jon had meetings, so I took the kids to the San Diego Zoo. My visit there did not hold the excitement of my initial discovery of it, but it was still an exciting place and Nigel enjoyed it with a three-year-old's fervor. I was uncomfortable when I found myself on isolated paths, but it was only sporadic. A man started walking with us, discussing photography. He was carrying the same kind of camera I was and said it was new, so he was asking questions. I tried to be polite in my coldness, but he soon realized I was not interested in his company. I felt good at the end of my day on my own.

The next day we headed for Death Valley for five days of camping. The first night we camped in the Funeral Mountains above the Valley and when night came a cold wind whipped through the camp. I was glad for the cold as it gave me the excuse to dress in heavy clothing, though our sleeping bags were very adequate for cold weather. I was uneasy, but I dismissed any serious fears.

The second night we camped in the Valley. We set up camp and drove off to explore the park. Death Valley held such fascination. Its message was time. Displaying its rocks that are thousands of millions of years old. As far away as a star, yet touchable.

When we returned to camp we found the campgrounds overflowing with young campers, mostly male. There were three men sitting at our picnic table who asked if they could share our campsite. They were hiking the Valley and there were no sites left when they arrived. How could we say no? We shared the table, but I did not join in the conversation. I avoided them, feeling very uncomfortable surrounded by strange men. I was suspicious of them all and couldn't be friendly. We went to bed as soon as the kids settled down, while the campground still pulsed with campfire conversations and music. Through the thin walls of the tent, shadows from the fires seemed to grow and voices came closer. The movements and sounds of people were all around us. We had been looking forward to this trip as an escape from tensions and an opportunity for togetherness. I hesitated in undressing, but I knew Jon had been waiting for this night—finally here and settled and the kids asleep. As I took off my clothes I felt a breeze. I felt so exposed, so public. I endured the intercourse but felt like a prostitute afterwards. Lying listening to the voices, feeling like "Who's next?" It was a nightmare. I didn't dare spoil Jon's evening by saying anything.

The next day we drove up to Red Mountain. We did

not see another car or person on the whole trip and I felt very secure at Jon's side. On Friday we explored some of the Valley canyons. We had just begun a hike up Mosaic Canyon when Nigel, in typical three-year-old fashion, declared, "I'm *so* tired. I can't even lift anymore feet." And he sat down to prove it. We decided I would sit with the kids at the mouth of the canyon while Jon walked up to explore, then he would watch them while I took my turn. As soon as I sat down, both kids were climbing all over the cliffs and running around, discovering crannies and creatures. "So tired, huh?" I mumbled. A group of two couples, one older and one younger, came up the trail. I heard the older man tell the others that he wasn't up to the hike and would wait for them. He sat down with me. I heard the voices of his group disappear up the canyon. The man started talking about his health and how he couldn't keep up with his son. He was divorced and trying to regain closeness with his teenager. I heard a lot of his life story before he landed on the Women's Lib topic.

"You certainly don't seem like that type. I'm sure you'd never try pushing men around. . . ."

I was clutching at my babes to keep them close to me. I had avoided conversation. I had gotten up and chased kids, paced, tried to move away from him, but he was persistent.

"Those two are hard to keep up with, aren't they?"

His words were too friendly, his movements too close. No one was nearby. There was only one escape route and I didn't even have car keys. I tried to talk the kids into walking with me up the canyon to meet Papa. Finally, Jon appeared.

I gritted my teeth to overcome the fears that would deprive me of seeing the canyon myself. I passed the son's group as I went up the trail. As the canyon narrowed and twisted, my imagination grew. I was afraid some man would meet me alone in the canyon without even a kid to clutch. I backed up to the solid-rock wall and wanted to scream just to release the tensions. The rocks, the air, the sky seemed to resent the intrusion of my life into their canyon. I turned and ran breathlessly back down the trail to my waiting family as the canyon closed in behind me.

"Whee, what a good trail for running on. All downhill."

"You sure are energetic for such a hot day!"

"Yeah." We walked back to the car.

With the weekend coming, we feared the campground would be even more crowded and the temperature had risen to 102°. Although we had to be back in San Diego in two days, we made a spontaneous decision to drive up to Yosemite. I did not regret leaving the Valley and looked forward to one night in a motel, with a tub and a locked door.

The Sierras were still covered with snow and the high lakes still frozen. Such a contrast to the 100° desert! To avoid the crowded areas on the Valley floor, we went to the Mariposa Redwood area to camp. There was distance between campsites and voices did not carry in the woods as they had in the desert. The 26° temperature that night sent everyone huddling inside tents early and again allowed me to hide in many layers of clothes. The fears that had been accumulating in Death Valley were muted in the beauty of Yosemite.

JOURNAL - May 1, Saturday

There is really a feeling of completeness in nature. The boundaries of myself are well defined. I exist as the trees and the hills around me exist. No more, no less. My body is the transportation of my mind. My mind is bigger than the universe and smaller than a spore. I am what is within me. I sat on a rock beside the road while Jon was out taking some photographs today. I sat with my back to the road. The sounds of cars passing became just another sound. I was not conscious of any other being. Some people hiked up from the lake. I watched them approach. Nothing more. No smile or jumping up for a greeting. No explanation of what I was doing. They were other creatures in the woods. It was acceptable behavior there. I can't just sit in our woods at home like that. We have to be *doing* something in our society. We must be social if someone approaches. At home humans are the world. Nature can't put us in perspective because there is no balance there. All other living things are just a doily on the table in suburbia.

It was harder than usual to leave California, but a clean house and new wallpaper made the homecoming more comfortable. It was fun to watch Nigel's excitement in rediscovering his toys. It was bedtime when I let down and realized how much I didn't want to be home. Too many thoughts, too many pressures, too many things I wanted to be away from and to forget.

JOURNAL - May 5, Wednesday
I want to go back to my rock in Yosemite. I'm not ready to face life. I don't even know what I don't want to face. I just want to retreat. Nights have been horrible since we got home. I lie awake with nightmares. I think of my assault and other rapes and I want to scream. I toss, I cringe, I thrash. I compose letters I want to write to complain to any-

one I can think of. I think of the first night, camping in Death Valley. Taking my clothes off in the tent, knowing all those men were just outside. All these haunting thoughts torturing my mind but I don't know why. The depression comes and goes during the day. I can be fine one minute then turn around to tears with nothing even to set them off. This morning was so bad. I didn't want to get up. I didn't want to face the day. I didn't want to see Mom who was coming to visit for the day. I cried in agony at being awakened. Jon stayed home to let me sleep late, thinking I was just too tired. He is so busy at work, he has so little patience left for me. I need him so much and can't stand to have him go away, yet when he is here he is so grouchy it is bad for both of us. I sit waiting in the evenings for him to come home. I don't even know what I want from him except for him to be home. Mom did come today and we had a pleasant chat. I felt very normal. When she left, I put the kids to nap and even felt inspired to get something done during their naptime but instead my depression snapped back.

Wish there was someplace I could go and scream till I was hoarse without people around. I should have done it in Mosaic Canyon. I might even have heard some echoes.

That evening I was sitting outside with a cup of coffee, watching the sunset as a tranquilizer, when a neighbor came over to welcome me home with the news that Sandy's house across the street had been burglarized. She was upset about it. I was a nervous wreck.

"You just never know where crime is going to hit. We're not as safe as we'd like to think we are. I was raped last October." I was talking to my coffee cup, not planning my sentences. I needed to tell someone at that moment. I needed to have someone shake with me in our vulnerability.

"You . . . ? Here?" Sue Ann spoke quietly, with uncertainty.

"Not in the house. I was outside. It's been a rough winter."

"Do any of the other neighbors know?"

"No. I haven't talked to anyone. I've been avoiding everyone. Things are getting better now."

"You don't have to worry. I won't say anything to anyone else. If you ever need to just talk, come over any time."

Why did people assure me they wouldn't tell anyone else? It made it sound so evil.

Later that week I saw Margot again. I didn't feel anything was resolved and was repressing tears when I left. Though the talk seemed unfinished, Margot had put some things together logically. Talking about my sex hang-ups, she saw a conflict between Victorian Me and Modern Me. She hypothesized how I was reared with Victorian attitudes imposed, and as soon as I was away from home, Free Me became dominant. Now the "Victorian Mother" was coming out of the closet and causing a new conflict.

JOURNAL - May 11, Tuesday

Another weird house dream. A contemporary house with an enchanting hidden bedroom, but as soon as I discovered all its charms I was told I wasn't allowed there.

Hot weather arrived and I was outside working on the yard when another neighbor, Rosa, leaned over her fence to chat.

"We just had our air conditioner repaired in time. It works so well now," she chatted.

"Hmmm. We need ours worked on too. It really isn't much help on these hot days."

"Well, the man that fixed ours has to come back tomorrow. I'll send him over to look at yours." I had never taken the course on How to Deal with Helpful Neighbors.

"Oh, no, I'd rather Jon be home when he comes—" I carefully arranged any maintenance visits for times when someone was with me and had even learned that I didn't have to answer the door for unexpected visitors.

"He'd probably just look at it and tell you what's wrong. He wouldn't have to do anything till you talked to Jon." She wasn't accepting the excuse I'd offered.

"No—it's—I'm afraid to have repairmen come when I'm alone at home—" I was tense. I stopped pulling weeds. Did I want to say it? She looked at me quizzically. "I was raped last October."

She paused before she reacted.

"At home?"

"No, outside."

"Did they catch the guy?"

"No."

"Was he black?"

"No." The question surprised me, but I realized that sooner or later many people had asked that question. I felt good to break the stereotype in her mind.

She shrugged her shoulders. "If you want the guy to look at your air conditioner, I'll come over with him."

She heard me; she accepted my fears. I was glad someone else knew. Once I decided to say it, it wasn't even very difficult. It was becoming an established fact.

Because I was still very tense and having trouble sleeping, Margot suggested I see a psychiatrist who could prescribe a tranquilizer for me. She recommended a woman who she thought was very good. When I went to my appointment with her, she arrived late. Maybe it was a sign that it had been a bad day for her, but she certainly turned it into a horrible day for me.

I followed her into her office and sat waiting uncomfortably as she arranged her papers in silence.

"Now. Can you describe your problem?"

"I . . . um . . . Well, I was raped last October and I'm having trouble sleeping and with nervousness again."

"Tell me about the rape." She was so cold, never a smile or a reaction. I felt as if I had to keep talking and that I wasn't saying things accurately because of the pressure to talk. She asked for details of the assault and when I had wrenched them out, she asked, "And that bothered you?" My God, what kind of answer did she expect to that question! How could a woman sit there and ask me if it bothered me to be raped! I felt as if I was talking to a computer filled with programmed questions. I wondered if she had ever even heard anything I said. I knew she didn't understand anything I said.

Finally she came to her conclusions. I should wean Colin so I could take antidepressant drugs. She didn't even know who I was, what I needed, and I didn't want antidepressants. If my heavy depressions continued, perhaps I would need that but I wasn't suicidal or nonfunctioning. And I didn't want to wean Colin. He would probably be our

last baby and I was happy to nurse him until he was ready
to quit. Nigel had had enough at sixteen months and Colin
seemed less interested than Nigel had been. I wanted to
continue that time of special togetherness with Colin. Besides, a crying toddler would not help my nerves. The
thought of weaning Colin because of the rape enraged me. I
was not willing to give up one of the few pleasures that had
survived the rape.

Her reaction to my adamant refusal to force Colin to
wean was a lecture on motherhood.

"You can't be a good mother if you're tense, so nursing
is no trade-off. Parents have to set the laws and not be run
by their children. Your happiness comes first. Playing the
martyr won't get you anyplace."

It was definitely not what I needed. She didn't know
anything about what kind of mother I was except that I
wanted to nurse my toddler. She made me feel like a textbook she was reading. I was depressed because I was still
feeling the effects of the rape. Her comment about why I
needed antidepressants was, "It's already been seven
months and you've got to get over this sometime!" Like I
should have forgotten it in a month. I was depressed because I felt no one listened to me and I didn't need absolute
proof to add to the fire! I finally got the prescription for a
tranquilizer in my hands and was able to get out the door
before the tears exploded.

JOURNAL - May 13, Thursday

Another house dream! This was a Victorian house I was trying to get organized in. It wasn't a dreary house, though
there were no windows. Very strange happenings of routine

business but I was definitely in charge of this house and I was comfortable there. The houses are me though, and it struck me how they are all either very modern or very Victorian as in Margot's description of the Victorian and the Modern me. It could almost make me believe in psychiatry.

I was able to express my feelings about the psychiatrist to Margot when I saw her the next week.

"Jennifer, I'm surprised. I'm really sorry it went so badly. I know you didn't need that now." She still had faith in the woman, but she didn't question my reaction to her. Perhaps there had been confusion; certainly there was no communication.

We talked about my inability to talk to people about my experience. I still felt threatened by other people because I didn't have all the questions settled in my mind. But I had told two people within a week and it wasn't as traumatic as I'd feared.

Things made sense when I talked to Margot. Often she didn't have to say anything. Sometimes I just heard myself.

On May 18 at 9:30 P.M., I got a call from a European friend who said he was flying in with a friend at 11 A.M. the next day. Jon had been corresponding with him about his visit, but I didn't know what the plans were. I didn't know if Jon could pick them up or if I'd have to, and Jon wasn't home that night to consult. I told him that someone would pick him up, but I didn't even know where they were planning to stay. I had thought he was going to visit us on the weekend, three days away. The house was a total mess, and if I had to pick him up at the airport, there would be no time to clean in the morning. I was up till midnight frantically cleaning. When Jon got home he said he'd pick them up and they would go sight-seeing all day and probably sleep downtown until Thursday. I scrubbed every corner just in case.

JOURNAL - May 19, Wednesday
I am really bitchy today. I know I'm tense about having company, especially two men staying here, one I've never even met before. I'm sure it is part of my motivation to have the house so clean. I'd like it to be spotless to show I'm in control. As if my house is my body—I take care of it and value it and it's not to be mistreated.

I survived the presence of the two male strangers in the house and was even relaxed with them as long as Jon was nearby. They were very pleasant and full of European courtesies. I spent a lot of time keeping the house spotless—as an American courtesy.

I took them to the bus station on Monday morning and declared the rest of the day "My Day." I took the kids to my mother's, and Michelle took the day off from work to join me for a day of exploring a quaint town nearby.

The weather was beautiful, the town was charming. We shopped and wandered but mainly talked. It was so rare that we had private times, like in the old days. We talked between shops and over coffee. Michelle brought up the topic of the rape as we ate our lunch in an outdoor cafe.

"It's such a lonely feeling when it happens," Michelle said. "Women should know how often it happens, that they're not alone." She had stopped eating as she concentrated on her words. "That's why I wanted to go to see you as soon as I found out. I was raped when I was eighteen."

"*You* were! My God, Michelle . . . !" I spilled my Coke as it left my mouth. My mind flipped back to the vacant hours of staring at the flowers on the wall that told me I was the only victim I'd ever met. God, my own sister-in-law!

"Actually it was just before you came home from college the Christmas after we graduated."

"When you were living with those three other girls on Eighteenth Avenue?"

"Yes. Remember Frank, the guy I dated for so long? When I was dating him . . . I went to meet him one night after work and a guy jumped into my car."

"I can't believe you never told me! Did you call the police?"

"No. It was strange. It was really horrible, but I felt stupid to have been in that part of town at that hour of the night. I didn't want my parents to know or they'd want me to move back home. They didn't want me living in the city anyway, remember? Frank was furious. He was ready to kill the guy. We broke up soon after that though. I didn't tell anyone else, but it didn't seem to affect me much except for breaking up with Frank. Things weren't the same. But I was more shaken up when it happened to you. God, that really shook me up. Maybe it's because we're older now. When I was eighteen, I didn't have a family that was dependent on me. It didn't seem to matter that much. Somehow it just didn't seem real then. I guess when it happened to you it brought a lot of the bitterness back. I've been paranoid since it happened to you. People might have suspected I had just been raped the way I was last fall.

"Want the other half of my sandwich?" she asked as she pushed her plate aside.

"No." We laughed and resumed our window shopping.

We ignored time, refusing to be pressured by rush hour traffic or waiting husbands. We felt young and free and warmed by our friendship.

It was so delightful to be able to smile again. That October walk seemed so far away. I still had fears and flashbacks, but they didn't control me. With time they were losing their intensity and frequency. I was learning to trust again, and I was opening up and finding it comfortable. My confidence had had its ups and downs but on a climbing scale, and I no longer felt different from other people. Finally I was caring about people more than I was fearing them, and I was learning my feelings weren't unique.

When I saw Margot again, we decided that I was able to make enough decisions and had enough confidence in my ability to cope alone, that we should skip the next appointment scheduled for June 3. I would check back with her in a month instead even though I didn't think that would be necessary.

JOURNAL - May 26, Wednesday

A fantastic dream today! It was very intense and I didn't understand it till I was telling Jon and heard what I was saying. It began in an auditorium mobbed with cheerful people where something evil was happening that only I was aware of. I struggled to get through the mobs, panicky because I knew "he" knew I was pursuing him. I tried to find Jon or Mom to take the kids to protect them. When I couldn't find them I took the kids with me, carrying Colin and clutching

Nigel so I wouldn't lose him. On a hill a man was preparing to make a TV statement and I saw the villain beside him. I knew that there was murder rigged to the TV camera but I couldn't get close enough to warn anyone. Just at the moment the camera was turned on, I willed the camera to turn toward the villain. A look of horror flashed on his face as he was sucked into the TV and when the crowd pulled him out, the top half of his body was a skeleton. Everyone was in shock over the horrible accident. I calmly walked away to find Jon as the mob dispersed. The dream was so grotesque, it surprised me that I could dream such a thing. When I was describing the middle-aged villain to Jon I suddenly saw who it was! Then it all made such sense. It was the scene of the last seven months. I resolved the situation in one dream and did away with the guy. The only flaw in the resolution was that his crime was never made public. He died with the world believing he was innocent, and he never had to face me or know that I was the cause of his death. He was simply done away with. At least half of him was done away with. Was that admitting that the real villain was his mind not his genitals or was it that I still haven't shaken the penis threat? It doesn't matter. The dream ended with satisfaction of a job completed. I really feel like I've finally gotten rid of it all so totally.

CHAPTER VII

"Hello, Mrs. Barr?"

"Yes?"

"This is Detective Jameson of the police department. We just picked up a suspect in your case and we're . . ."

"A suspect?" I needed to slow him down, to confirm the news I'd given up waiting for.

"A man who fits the description you gave us. We'd like for you to come in to view a lineup if you could, on Tuesday at seven?"

"Next Tuesday? Yes, that's O.K."

"We'll have maybe six or seven men in the lineup for you to look at to identify the man who assaulted you. They won't be able to see you though. Someone from the State's attorney's office and the suspect's attorney will also be there.

I'll be there to explain the procedure to you. Do you have any questions now about it?"

"No, not yet. But when it sinks in, I may."

"Well just call me back if you do. Try not to worry about it now."

"Right now I'm just excited."

"Don't get hopes up too high. It's been seven months. Could be someone else. It could be hard to remember. . . ."

"I remember!" I said confidently.

"Good, I hope so. Hope you have a pleasant weekend and call if you have questions, O.K.?"

"O.K."

It was Friday, May 28, 2 P.M. I put the receiver gently on the hook and sat down. *Had they really caught him? After all this time!* I tried to call Rosemary, needing someone to tell me what was happening. She wasn't home. I tried to slow my mind down to think of what it meant immediately rather than the possible implications. I called Margot's office to schedule an appointment for the next week, realizing I might be needing some emotional support by then. Fortunately the appointment time that I had canceled the week before was still open. I set up a baby-sitter for Tuesday night. I called Karen.

"Hi, Karen. This is Jennifer. Do you have anything on your schedule for Tuesday night?" Karen had become a Rape Crisis counselor and I wanted someone from the Center there to help me keep up with what was going on.

"Um, let's see, Tuesday? No, it's clear so far. What's up?"

"Oh, just a lineup."

"A lineup! For your case? Are you kidding?"

"No, a real live lineup. Jameson just called. It's so unreal. They have a suspect. What do you know about lineups?"

"Nothing at all. Listen, I was just on my way out when you called. I'm really excited and want to talk but would it be O.K. to call you back later? Tuesday night is fine and I'm glad you called me. I feel rotten, dashing off on you. What time is it on Tuesday?"

"Seven, I think, or is it seven-thirty? Yugh, I don't remember that detail."

"Don't worry about it, we'll find out. Call you later, O.K.?"

"Sure, that's O.K."

I felt efficient when I finished my phone calls. Everything was arranged but nothing was settled. Rosemary still wasn't home.

I went next door to Rosa. "Hi. I need to have a cup of coffee with you. The police just called and said there's going to be a lineup on Tuesday, and I'm a nervous wreck. . . ."

"C'mon in. I was just baking a birthday cake and the coffee's hot. Do you know a good recipe for fudge frosting? That's what he wants."

We were in different worlds but I just needed company.

JOURNAL - May 28, Friday

This is unreal. It's all here again. Now when I've finally begun to table it. Especially even this week after the dream I had last Wednesday. Seeing him on Tuesday he won't be a skeleton again. My thinking and reactions will change heavily. And what if it's not the guy? What a letdown after

thinking of it all weekend. And if it is, then the next steps—
hearings, trial, etc. Am I up to that? Together enough now?
What if I have doubts in identifying him? That would be
the worst thing, if I'm not *sure*. I feel pretty confident that I
can identify him except that when I saw him he wore the
hat and sunglasses and was very tense. Without his disguise,
and looking passive, will he be recognizable?

It was Memorial Day weekend and I was glad we
had a busy weekend planned. Tuesday seemed a long way
off. I was anxious to get it over with, to know if it was the
right guy or not, to know if I did remember enough to identify him. I was filled with so many doubts and questions that
could not be answered till Tuesday. I was filled with nervous energy that needed a use.

Saturday morning I put more effort than usual into the
picnic we had planned with Bart and Sarah. We hadn't seen
much of our old friends and I wanted to relax and enjoy the
visit, but my mind kept coming back to the same thoughts.
We had told them about the assault when we saw them at
Christmas but hadn't talked much about it. I was usually
able to escape from my thoughts with them, ideas and phi-
losophies were interesting, safe topics.

On that Saturday neither tectonic-plate theory nor the
Alaskan wilderness could command my attention. I drew
Sarah aside and told her my news as soon as I had a chance.
After I explained my jitters to Bart too, I felt open to talk
about the thoughts that popped in my mind. They were
both interested in hearing it all and were very accepting and
understanding about my state of mind that day.

Sunday started with church where I was anxious to tell

Ava the news. Ava often still asked if I'd heard anything yet, so I was anxious to say "Yes!" I burst upon her with the news. I wasn't concerned for once about who might witness or overhear.

"They have a suspect! They picked up someone." I clutched her arm as I talked. "There'll be a lineup on Tuesday night."

"Oh, Jennifer, I think of you every day and get so mad that I don't call. I'm so busy with co-op and church and family. They take so much time. Can I come over on Tuesday? Hang everything else!"

"Oh yes, Ava. It may be a very long day."

When I told Pastor he looked at me blankly, his mind was someplace else. I didn't know if I should repeat myself or explain. Finally his eyes softened as he said, "I'll be thinking about you on Tuesday."

That afternoon was the neighborhood Memorial Day picnic. The holiday get-togethers were good opportunities for meeting new neighbors and visiting with old. They could be tedious, depending on the amount of beer consumed or which neighbors were feuding. They could be pleasant. I was not in the mood for socializing for socializing's sake, but I was glad for the time filler. Though I tried to stay near the neighbors who knew what was going on so that I wouldn't need to hide my nervousness, a new neighbor introduced herself to me.

"Hi. I'm Nancy. We moved in the Johnsons' house last November. I hear you have two sons. I have a two-year-old boy too. How old are yours? . . . I'm so glad there'll be someone for Bryan to play with. We'll have to get together soon. How long have you lived here? Are you from this area originally? I'm from New York, cancha' tell."

Though I wasn't very responsive, I tried to be polite. Finally I made an excuse to go inside. I didn't want to make a bad impression.

JOURNAL - May 31, Monday

I am pretty scared tonight. I've been pretty calm today but suddenly it hit me—tomorrow is the day. I have stage fright. "What am I doing anyway?" I've gone over and over this in my mind just as an actor rehearses, and here on the eve of the performance I suddenly question my ability to come through. I don't know what I'm afraid of but it just doesn't seem like this is all going to really happen.

On Tuesday I couldn't get my mind off the lineup. I wrote lists of the features I remembered, thought about how he could have changed in seven months, thought about unchangeable features. I was very concerned about being correct in my identification. I didn't think I would accuse the wrong man, though that was possible. If I picked out someone who was not the suspect, my credibility in any future lineups would be questionable. My greatest fear was that I wouldn't recognize him, and he would be set free. I tried to think of all the possibilities. I made calls to learn as much as I could about the legal procedure and legal implications. I talked to Detective Jameson. I was worried about the defense attorney. Could he ask me questions? Did I have to answer him? Could he use things I said in court?

"No. The defense attorney is just a private citizen and can ask all he wants, but you have no obligation to answer.

He is only there to be sure it is a fair lineup. Someone from the State's attorney will be there to protect you."

I called Carol at the Crisis Center, trying to learn as much as I could about the legal process and consequences. The police were very helpful, but to them it was a routine procedure, and they couldn't understand how frightening it was for someone whose legal comprehension stopped with "Perry Mason," TV version.

Ava spent the afternoon with me. Her presence more than the chatter helped cushion the time. I tried to nap after she left, but I couldn't even lie down. Supper came and I forced some casserole down, knowing if I didn't eat I'd be sick with nerves. When everyone else finished eating, I quit too.

A storm was ready to break outside. The sky was dark and suddenly the wind started. The rain came quite suddenly, without the typical scattered warning drops. The rain came in torrents. What horrible weather for venturing out. Jon and I had decided it might be easier if I went alone with Karen. My nervousness made Jon nervous and cycled back to make me more nervous. Karen was late arriving to pick me up, and I stood silently at the window watching the rain as I waited.

As we drove to the police station, the storm cleared and a rainbow appeared spanning the highway.

"Oh, Karen, that's too obvious to be a good omen, isn't it?"

"At this point your nerves need all the good omens they can get. Take it." We laughed. It was a beautiful rainbow.

We were the first to arrive at the police station and waited until Detective Jameson showed us into a large meeting room. Other people were arriving by that time and the next person in the room was a woman I knew.

"Bev! What are you doing here!"

"Jennifer!"

Detective Jameson interrupted us.

"I'm sorry, but you're not permitted to talk about your cases."

We looked at each other in disbelief. She was a friend I had met soon after we moved to the area and one I saw off and on. There we were in the same situation of waiting to view a lineup. Was she a victim too? Perhaps a witness? I'd have to wait to find out.

I chain-smoked and wondered about the other people there. There was some talk, mainly about the weather. There was a young man who talked enough to say he was a jewelry salesman. All the other people were women. A teenage girl looked the right age to be the girl who had been grabbed and escaped two weeks before me. There was another woman there with a ten- or eleven-year-old girl.

Detective Jameson briefed us on the procedure. He introduced the woman from the State's attorney's office and the defense attorney. The defense attorney, Mr. Canfield, did not present a pleasant image. It looked as if he considered the whole procedure an insult.

The woman with the young girl asked if she could accompany her daughter. "I wouldn't say anything. She's scared and wants me with her."

"That should be O.K." Jameson said.

"She can't do that!" Canfield snarled.

"Well, let's talk about it in the hall when I finish briefing them."

"I want this settled right now. No one is supposed to influence the procedure. She's got to identify him and no one else."

"We'll settle it later." Gentle Jameson had a firm side too and he continued despite Canfield's sulking.

I was the first witness called in. I followed Detective Jameson as he led me into a dark room. I steeled my nerves to tackle the task at hand. My eyes were immediately drawn to the lighted line of six middle-aged men standing beyond a glass wall. I had hoped that I could spot him immediately if he were there. I didn't. I stood studying each one for possibilities. My knees felt like jelly. They all looked like anybody's uncle or the local insurance agents. Ms. Parrish, the State's representative, asked if I wanted to sit. I did. My knees could not have held me much longer.

"Do you want a cigarette?"

"No." I was concentrating too hard. I was afraid if I relaxed for a moment I would fall apart.

I eliminated one man immediately as too old. They turned for a side view. I studied each man carefully for any familiarity. They each put on a hat and sunglasses. One remained as a possibility. I knew the features I was looking for. His general appearance fit, but I needed to see more than a deadpan expression to be sure. They asked if I had any postures to request. I asked if they could open their mouths.

"You mean yawn?" the defense attorney sneered.

"No, just relax their jaws—breathe through their mouths."

"How about if they say something?" Jameson suggested.

"O.K."

"What do you want them to say?" someone asked.

"Anything. It doesn't matter."

Someone made a suggestion, but Ms. Parrish suggested it should be something he said during the assault.

"Can you think of something he said?"

I thought for a while. I couldn't recall seeing him as he said anything.

"No."

"You don't remember anything he said?" the defense lawyer asked incredulously.

"Oh yes. I remember things he said, but I didn't see him say them." *I'm not your run-of-the-mill dingaling, mister!*

"Just have them repeat anything you heard. You'll have to say it later anyway," advised Ms. Parrish. She had a soft mature voice for such a young petite appearance.

"Well . . . O.K. . . . Have them say . . . 'Take off your clothes.'"

As we talked I watched the second man. He put his head back and took a deep breath through his mouth. I saw his downturned mouth, his small jaw and uneven nostrils. God, is that him? That worm that looks so normal? I was too far away to check for the identifying scar on the side of his face, but the grotesque face that still plagued me provided enough distinct features that I did not need the scar for identification.

When he spoke, an electric current ran down my spine turning the dark room into an autumn woods.

"Anything else?"

"No."

As I walked out I was handed a clipboard with a form. "Circle the number and check positive, possible, or none and sign your name."

"#2—positive." I signed it and dropped the board. Ms. Parrish touched my hands and said, "Relax . . . go home and write up as much as you can remember about it all. It helps."

"I have . . . I have . . ." and I crumbled. The sobs came. Someone passed me going into the lineup room. Was it Bev who saw me sobbing? Detective Jameson suggested we go to a back room and sit down with some coffee. Karen was there. I never looked up until we were seated and the sobs quieted.

"He was so little. He looked so docile, so mild, so harmless standing there under the lights. Could he possibly have done that to me?"

"Jennifer, you said you were positive. Are you saying you're not sure now?"

"God, Karen, I'm sure. I can't believe it, but I am sure."

The flashbacks kept hitting, juxtapositioned with that ordinary-looking man. While talking to Karen, my mood would lighten, then it would hit me again. Jameson came in twice to offer help. A policewoman came in and sat down to talk. She said that he was picked up last week at the lake after one more episode there that sounded like the same guy. She had gone out to the lake the next day as a decoy with patrolmen in the wings. He was there, acted suspiciously and fit the description. She said the next step would be that the State's attorney's office would contact me, but she had no idea how long it would be.

JOURNAL - June 1, Tuesday

Three gin and tonics and I barely feel it. Maybe a bit of extra adrenalin flowing here. God, what a night. What do I say even. So much yet so little can be put into words.

What if I did make a mistake? I'm human. What if I was positive about the wrong man? How could he have done such evil? He looked so normal. Why am I so horribly upset?

The next few days were filled with flashbacks of the attack. It seemed as if it had just happened. Seeing him made it all real again. I was glad I had had the foresight to reschedule my appointment with Margot as soon as Jameson called. I was exploding with emotions, with tears erupting on and off for no apparent reason. I couldn't identify my feelings—fears, anger, excitement were all mixed together, bombarding my mind.

On Wednesday Jon stayed home to let me sleep late. Soon after I woke up, Nancy came to the door, collecting for some charity. I was still groggy from sleep and asked Jon to take care of it. I felt guilty at being so unfriendly to a new neighbor who was obviously making an effort to be neighborly.

When Jon left for work, I got on the phone. I needed to talk. I tried to call Rosemary but she was out. I called Karen. We had a long talk about what had happened and what would happen next. She was good to talk to. She always reinforced my confidence just when I felt I was losing control. We talked about the Crisis Center in general and about future training sessions. She mentioned a recent trainee who lived on my street—Nancy! I couldn't believe it.

The irony. How I'd hidden my nervousness from her, avoiding her that very morning.

I was anxious to talk to Nancy, to Bev, to Ava, to Rosemary, and I kept trying to call each of them and they were all out. Rosemary finally called and we had a long conversation. I jumped from topic to topic irrationally, but it was O.K.

Then I tried to call Bev again. Her husband answered.

"She's not here. Can I take a message?"

"Yes, this is Jennifer. . . ."

"Jennifer? Oh, wait a minute, I'll get her." She had been at the lineup as a witness to an indecent-exposure case. She hadn't identified a suspect though. "They all fit the general description. I didn't think I could pick anyone out anyway. It was all so quick. What were you a witness for?"

"Rape. . . . I was the victim."

"Jennifer! When?"

"October."

"You've been carrying that inside you all this time! Oh, Jennifer, I never could have guessed. You of all people!"

"Yeah. That's what I always said—me of all people!" I found it easier to admit now. I knew it was real, not my imagination—that it all did happen.

After supper I called Karen again to see if she had learned anything from the police yet.

"Well, I couldn't get hold of Jameson for details, but I found out he is still being held in jail."

"In jail?"

"Yeah. I think they really want to get him, and they must have enough evidence now to be pretty sure they've got the right guy."

"Somebody must have identified him at the lineup. Wish I could find out the results of it. Was he identified by any others? Wonder if Jameson would even tell us."

"I don't know, but I'll keep trying to see what I can find out."

JOURNAL - June 2, Wednesday, A.M.

Is it all on my identification? What a scary thought. Hopefully someone else identified him at least as a possibility. They only had fleeting looks at him. They didn't study him like I did. Could I have made a mistake? Maybe it's not even on my identification. I certainly don't think I was mistaken but there is that shadow of doubt—not rational doubt, just "what if . . ." doubt. Oh that is too scary to think about. I was very careful. I am sure. But what if . . . ?

After talking to Karen, I called Nancy to tell her first that I wasn't coming to her Tupperware Party that night and second why I wasn't up to going. She had known the whole thing for quite a while and had wanted to meet me and talk to me but didn't know what approach to use. The way she had gotten involved in the Center was through her close friend Doris. "My" counselor even! What an irony! She had come to the picnic solely to meet me! She came down to say hello and to meet Jennifer Barr. She was so glad I'd called her; she had hoped sooner or later I'd hear about her and take the initiative.

Finally enough time off the phone to get the kids in bed and Ava called. I must have talked on the phone for six hours that day, and my day started at noon! Everyone was so concerned. I felt so close to so many people. I'd never felt

such a "community of concern." It was certainly a good day
to build my faith and trust in people.

Nigel overheard some of the phone conversations and
asked about something he overheard about the assault, so I
explained to him what was going on. Obviously he was
aware I was nervous, and it was unusual for me to be on the
phone so much. It was not surprising that he asked. I explained to him that I had been attacked, the police had
caught the man, and last night I had to identify him so they
would put him in jail.

"I would catch the man and kill him, but first I'd make
him little. I'd make him into a spider and smash him and
throw him out of his house so he couldn't attack you!"

*My little wonderful protector. What a wonderful child
you are!* It made me wish that I had talked to him about it
before, but there is a big difference in his comprehension at
age three and what he could have understood seven months
earlier. He knew that something bad had happened, and it
seemed better to tell him rather than let it fester in his imagination. But I worried about his interpretation of the situation; his imagination could take hold of facts as easily as
fiction!

JOURNAL - June 2, Wednesday, P.M.

The story of the man being arrested was on the front page
of the county paper. A few facts were distorted. I was described as a "seventeen-year-old." I knew this was all
unreal. It didn't happen to me—it was a seventeen-year-old.
The other descriptions of the victims were wrong too. The
headlines carried a rather strange slant. Said "Man Charged
With Indecent Exposure." Later in the article, paragraph

four, it added "also accused of assault, rape and perverted sex acts by a seventeen-year-old resident." Do I detect a slant of disbelief or am I being hypersensitive? Oh well. But there was his name, age, and address. Like a real person. It's hard to believe he committed all of his crimes at the same place, wearing the same disguise, always on warm sunny days. Did he really think he'd never be caught?

I'm still so wound up. I wonder how long it will be till I hear from the State's attorney's office. I feel myself waiting like I did last October. Waiting to hear, waiting for something to happen. Nothing I can do. It may be a few days. It may be weeks before I hear anything. So glad Karen is trying to find out what's happening and keeping me informed. So glad I'm seeing Margot tomorrow. I keep juxtaposing that ordinary "little" man with the gorilla kneeling on top of me, holding my head with intense hatred. God, how can a human be so vicious! Could that guy standing in the lineup have been capable of threatening my existence? He might have killed me and there he stood, looking so normal, so powerless, so scared.

Thursday turned into an intense day despite my graspings for control. I tried to plan, to think, to keep calm. In the morning I was restless and wanted company, so I asked Nancy to come over. I told her why I wanted to see her. "I'm a nervous wreck. I just need company." She said she'd come as soon as she got ready. I called Rosemary to fill the time. At about eleven o'clock, two hours after I called Nancy, she called back.

"Listen, I have a problem with another rape victim that I need to take care of today. Can you baby-sit my kid?"

"Oh . . . I have a one-o'clock appointment with Margot."

"That's O.K. Listen, I'll call Doris and she can pick him up from you as soon as she's free. I just can't get hold of her right now. I'm sure she'll be home by noon. That'll give you time, O.K.?"

"O.K."

I was upset as soon as I hung up. Why had I said yes, or had I? I had told her I needed help, but not only did she not come through with help but added an extra child that I didn't even know. Why had she even asked when I'd told her I was upset? It was a bad start.

I called the only neighbor who was home, Sandy, whom I'd had to lunch in October and who still didn't know anything about my situation. I was getting desperate.

"Sandy? I need company. Can you come over for a bit?"

"Sure." She didn't ask for any explanation.

I put the coffee on to heat and sat watching for her. She and Nancy appeared at the same moment. As I went to the door I heard the coffee begin to boil over. Bryan stood in the doorway, crying, as Nancy explained:

"I'm sorry to leave him like this, but I have to take this victim over to see Margot. She's really upset and so I need to take her. I really appreciate your taking Bryan. Gotta run."

Sandy was already inside as I turned to comfort Bryan, and the phone rang. It was Jon on the phone, so I got off easily and sat down at the table. Bryan was still by the door but had stopped crying when Nigel and Colin went to meet him.

"Sandy, you wouldn't believe what's been going on here. I'm not sure I know. Let me get us some coffee."

"Well, my God, this place is a circus right now. There's more to the story than this?"

"Oh, Sandy, there's been a lot hiding behind these doors. I was raped last October."

"Wha . . ." Her coffee rocked with the table. She wasn't a person who hid her feelings.

"Yeah, the week before you came here for lunch, matter of fact. That was seven months ago and last week they picked up a suspect and Tuesday there was a lineup and here I am in pieces again."

"Was it him? My God, does anyone else know? I'd have been a raging lunatic long ago. Where have I been? And I've been so upset over our robbery. God, how have you stayed sane?"

"Oh, Sandy." I sighed to hear someone else emote so strongly on the matter. "I haven't stayed so sane. Your burglary really set me off too. I think I probably reacted about as strongly as you did to it. I'd just begun telling people about it. I really couldn't talk about it for so long."

"Does anyone else in the neighborhood know?"

"Rosa and Sue Ann. I told Sue Ann right after your break-in. It's only been in the last couple weeks."

She was filled with questions and I was relieved to find someone I could talk to openly about the event and its aftermath. The visit was too short though. She had an appointment so had to leave, but I was glad she was the neighbor who happened to be home at the moment I needed a neighbor.

Soon after she left, Doris came to pick up Nancy's son.

"How are you doing?" she asked as she wiped Bryan's running nose.

"Falling apart, thank you. It's just all coming down on me again," I told her honestly.

She stood up and sighed and, without looking at me, said, "Don't worry. There is nothing to be upset about at this point."

It didn't console me. It made me feel as if I was over-reacting. Feeling on the verge of an explosion was no time to be told there's nothing to be upset about.

As Doris was leaving, Ava stopped by with a smile and some lettuce from her garden. She left her car running so she wouldn't stay. It said more than a long visit. Even though she had no time at all, she stopped to show she was thinking of me!

I put the kids to nap and finally had a moment of peace before going to see Margot. A moment to compose myself. I hadn't wanted to be alone that morning, but I didn't need Grand Central Station either.

Jon came home to baby-sit the kids while I kept my appointment. He was late, so I had to dash and arrived late and breathless. The secretary asked me to wait as Margot had another client with her. Ten minutes passed. It was unusual for Margot to be late. The secretary finally gave her a ring to be sure she hadn't lost track of time. Margot came out to see me.

"Hi, Jennifer"—in her always cheerful voice—"there's really been some confusion here today. I thought we'd canceled your appointment this week and I scheduled someone else in."

I burst into tears. I'd been hanging on to see Margot.

Now what? Make an appointment for next week? Suddenly everything fell apart.

"Jenn, Jenn, listen. I'll find you a place to wait and I'll see you in fifteen to twenty minutes, O.K.? Can you hang in there that long? Can I get you some coffee? I'm so sorry this happened."

"Yes . . . yes. I don't know what's wrong. . . . I can wait. . . . I feel so silly. . . . This is so dumb. . . ." I rubbed impatiently at the tears on my cheeks.

As I waited in a vacant office I thought I'd finally flipped out. I kept crying, alternating with angry words, at my tears. *What the hell is happening? Why am I so upset? What do I say to Margot anyway?* I tried to read the posters on the walls, but they wouldn't make sense either. I tried to laugh at my misreading the words, but it was a forced laugh. *You've really cracked this time.* I fantasized about what would happen to me. What would happen when I saw Margot. *No, I'll never leave this room. People will still come and use this office and never even know I'm here. The clients will have to sit on my lap to find out about the Senior Citizens' Dial-a-Ride services. I wonder if the master of this office will miss the Kleenex? How can she function here, knowing a mind disappeared in this room? Maybe she'll find it and wonder who it belongs to. Well, I don't want it back, thank you. I'm perfectly happy being a chair.* I began to hope Margot would not return for me. That I could stay there when the building closed up for the night. Maybe the whole world could lose me. Maybe I should leave and really disappear. Where would I go? What could I say to Margot? What could she say to me?

"Gads, Jennifer, it sounds like your emotions have suddenly all fired at the same time, and you haven't had time to sort out any of them."

"Yes, Margot. I guess that's it, must be."

"Can we try to work on one at a time?"

"We can try, Margot."

Margot didn't give me any magic answers, but it helped to ease my mind to hear her say she thought my state of mind was understandable. I was trying to contain many conflicting feelings, and until one side won out, I would have to have patience with the confusion. We went back to a weekly appointment schedule.

When I got home I felt calmed enough to call the State's attorney's office to see if I could get some answers from Ms. Parrish to end some of my suspense.

"Oh yes, Mrs. Barr. I'm so glad you finally called. I've been waiting to hear from you after you'd had a chance to get yourself back together. I'm so glad you were able to let out your emotions. It's a healthy reaction. It's always dangerous to bottle things up. So often witnesses can get turned around when they are fighting their emotions. I'm glad you're not letting this get you down. You did a good job on Tuesday."

"Was he identified by the others?"

"No, but you see you were the prime witness anyway. The others didn't see him as well, but we're proceeding on all three cases. I'm sure it's the same man."

"Well, what happens next? Is he in jail now?"

"He's being held on $110,000 bond so I don't think we need to worry. He's not going to be able to post that kind of money. We've got a good case on this guy, so don't worry.

The next step will be a preliminary hearing which is a formality to set the charges."

"When will that be?"

"Should be in a few days, probably Monday. But don't worry, you don't have to attend. I'll keep in touch with you about it."

JOURNAL - June 3, Thursday

$110,000. God, somebody is serious about this. How could they have such a high bail just on one identification? $110,000. God.

CHAPTER VIII

I DON'T remember what he said as he stood to heat the coffee after supper. It wasn't his words as much as his timing that set off my tears.

"What's the matter, Jenn? What did I say?" The harder I tried to explain to Jon, the harder the sobs came. I felt alone, desperately alone. I was suddenly unsure of everything. I wanted it all to go away. I couldn't accept the responsibility. I couldn't face the future. I wailed hysterically. The kids were out playing, the dishes sat on the table, the doors and windows were all open. I escaped farther and farther from the kitchen table as my face, smeared with tears, pressed into it. Jon lifted my head and tried to hold me. Trees might hear, but they don't respond. I stared at the air in front of me.

"Has she said anything to you?"

"No, she has been just sitting like this since before I called you. I've talked to her, but she won't respond. I'm sorry to call you out tonight, but I didn't know what to do, Margot."

They discussed what had been said that evening, what might have set her off.

"One hundred and ten thousand dollars."

"What's $110,000, Jennifer?" Margot's face was very close and she spoke slowly and calmly.

"Everyone wants to get him . . . everyone. . . . They really want to get him. . . ."

"How do you feel about it, Jennifer?"

"Oh . . . oh, the dishes still on the table . . . I've got to get the kids to bed. Jon, it's so dark!" And I started crying quietly again. Reality was too confusing.

"Jenn, I already put the kids to bed. They are in bed and asleep."

"Jennifer, there are some responsibilities that others can help you with. You're not alone. You don't have to go through with this if you don't want to."

"I have to, Margot. Everyone has put so much work into it. I couldn't let everyone down."

"Jenn, if you can't do it, they'll understand. They don't have as much at stake as you do. You don't have to."

"Yes . . . I do have to. I won't understand if I can't." I knew it was my choice. I knew it was my own expectations and requirements that told me I had to pursue the case. It was my choice to accept the responsibility.

Margot spelled out a plan for me to get through the next day. "Plan your day very strictly and schedule a time to be depressed." We worked out an hour-by-hour schedule which I first disrupted by sleeping late and finally abandoned with Jon's suggestion that we go to a craft fair. It provided a very relaxed escape. I became thoroughly absorbed in the creativity and inspired by ideas I gathered.

On the drive there and back, I had the time for quiet thinking. Thoughts came more gently. I considered the lineup in a controlled light. I had done my best and should be proud of my identification. I had gone in as prepared as possible, with full knowledge of my responsibilities. I could not accept responsibility for the accused; his future was out of my hands. If I had made a mistake, certainly the court would clear him. If he was guilty but released in spite of my best efforts, I still had accomplished something. He was in jail now and he was known to the police. It had been a lucky fluke that I had thought to study him carefully at the time of the attack. It was a luckier fluke that the police had found him seven months later. I felt relieved and tried not to worry about the future.

In spite of my more orderly mind, I was still nervous and shaky. At church that Sunday I did a lot of contemplating. The sermon on human frailty was well timed. I was glad to be reminded that I was human and my responsibility was limited to what I perceived as truth, that perfect truth and justice were out of the human realm.

My thoughts lingering on the sermon were interrupted by people turning to clasp neighbors' hands in welcome. I was made aware of the people around me and I was not ready for it. I was too much within my world to reach out. I was afraid someone would turn to enter my world and see my awkwardness. I held my head down and fumbled, but suddenly a hand was on my arm. Ava had come to me from across the aisle and grasped my hand.

"I can see what you're going through and my heart is with you." My tears surfaced as she spoke and I kissed her, instinctively, without embarrassment. It was a beautiful spontaneous moment, and I felt part of the world again.

Monday arrived at 5 A.M. when I awoke, feeling very alert and needing to take advantage of the tranquillity of early morning. I heard the first bird chirp and gradually the chorus beginning to announce the coming of the sun. The treetops were filled with songs, and a dove's coo came from deeper in the woods. Only the occasional sound of a distant car made man's presence obvious. As I went deeper into the morning sounds, I sensed a constant undefined hum of more distant traffic. I sat for two hours, watching the ants on the patio and the birds in the grass. It was the unhurried time I needed for thinking. The whole incident unraveled in my head. Calmly, step by step, I relived and examined the assault. I remembered details I hadn't recorded before. I felt confident that I could handle a legal battle. I also felt a need to review the renewed memories that had surfaced with the lineup. I wanted to talk to an attorney while it was still fresh.

It was a good beginning for the day. I was relaxed and ready for the family when they awoke. We all had a cheerful breakfast together.

Later in the day I visited Rosemary, and we walked to the playground with the children. She had asked to read the report of the rape I'd written for the police, so I took it along that day. I wasn't embarrassed to show it to her as she had already heard all the details over the past eight months, but it seemed so clinical in black and white. I had recorded everything that I saw, heard, smelled, or felt that morning. I had recorded every movement that I could remember of the assailant and his victim. The short sentences, each beginning with "He" or "I," had the rhythm of a bass drum in a slow march. It had been written without emotion; it had been written to include every detail and every possible clue for the police.

Though Rosemary had known about the report since the night I wrote it, she had never asked to see it. At this point of renewed intensity, she asked. I did not see any reason to refuse her request.

I didn't watch her as she read it and waited until she said something before I turned my attention back to her.

"Are you upset that you read it?"

"No . . . and yes. I feel different."

"But there wasn't anything new, was there?"

"No, nothing new. It was just . . . all together. Step by step. I hadn't thought of it like that. I don't know why it's different. It's almost ordinary . . . no, cold . . . no, you know, like it just happened. Like it happened so . . . so . . . like it could have been me."

As we walked back I chattered about different topics, feeling awkward with her unusual quietness. We sat at her picnic table with coffee, both feeling frustrated over our loss of words. I wanted to know what was behind her subdued mood, and she seemed frustrated with the intensity of emotions that she was unable to express. I didn't push her though; in fact, I had put up a glass wall to observe her through. We both realized it was pointless to continue our visit. I left her to her own thoughts.

When I got home, I called the State's attorney's office to speak to Ms. Parrish about what was happening with the preliminary hearing.

"Oh, it's not till Thursday. Don't worry about it."

"Well, the lineup brought all this stuff back, and I'd like to go over it with the attorney."

"I'd be glad to see you about it if it would ease your mind. I can't see any problems with the hearing. We've really got a case on this guy."

"Well, I would like to talk to someone so I know what's going on."

"Sure. Fine. How about tomorrow at two?"

Pastor called that afternoon.

"I just talked to Ava. I didn't realize the trauma you've had with last week's events. I should have known. I just didn't think. I should have called earlier."

"Well, I'm glad you called anyway. Thank you for your concerns."

"I'd really like to talk to you. We haven't talked for a while, and it's still going on, isn't it?"

"Yes, on and off . . . and now on again."

"I didn't realize how traumatic this has been. I should have known. Can I call you on Friday to talk?"

"Yes, or why don't you stop over. It's easier than the phone."

"I'm glad you said that. I didn't want to intrude, but I'd really like to talk to you. Thank you."

"O.K. See you on Friday at about one? That's still the best time for me—kids' naptime."

It must have been a difficult call for him. He was obviously feeling awkward. His sentences seemed well re-

hearsed. They were punctuated by embarrassment and
guilt. I had noticed the absence of any comments from him
and was beginning to lose faith in him, so I was glad he
called. I was relieved it was lack of knowledge not lack of
concern. After all, why should he automatically know? I had
hinted that the lineup was significant but nothing more. I
expected people to show concern, but it was difficult for me
to tell them I needed support. It was easy to see how the
awkward situation developed and I felt sorry for the embarrassment I'd caused Pastor. I hoped we would have a good
talk on Friday to clear the air.

I was let down the next day after seeing Ms. Parrish.
She only wanted to brief me on what was going on and give
me a chance to feel at ease with her. I had been preparing
myself to tell the whole story, and she hadn't planned to
hear it. She showed me the courtroom—the judge's bench,
the jury box, the tables for defendant and prosecution. It
looked very unpleasant. My knees were shaky as I sat in
the witness chair and tried to imagine the unimaginable.

She took time to explain the charges. Rape, assault with
intent to commit rape, perverted sexual acts, and assault and
battery.

"He's still being charged with rape? Even though
there's no medical exam?"

"That shouldn't be a problem."

"But what evidence is there for rape?"

"Your testimony. At the preliminary hearing, the lack
of a medical report will be explained. It might get hung up
there, but I don't think so. How was it that there's no medical
report?"

"The officer asked if I wanted to go to the hospital and

I didn't see any reason to. I wasn't hurt and I couldn't get pregnant. Besides I'd had sex with my husband that morning anyway. . . ."

"I've gotta warn you. The new sexual assault laws will go into effect next month, so you'll be covered by it. It's to your advantage 'cause it means they can't bring up any of your sexual history, but it also means you can't mention sex with your husband. The part about nursing your baby is inadmissible too."

"Nursing my baby! That's not sexual. Nor history."

"But it has nothing to do with the rape."

"But if I'm asked what I said to him, I said . . ."

"It could be grounds for a mistrial."

It was difficult to accept. If I was supposed to tell the truth at this trial, how could I omit any part of it? Pick and choose the facts? The law didn't seem to carry much logic. It did not occur to me then that perhaps Ms. Parrish was not qualified to interpret the laws.

She proceeded to explain other laws and procedures I should be aware of—delays in trial dates, sequestering, defense techniques.

"Most people don't understand about all this stuff. I've been working as a paralegal long enough that I've seen a lot of this happen. Don't worry about it though. We had one case here where . . ." She went into details of past cases and got quite carried away with her descriptions and judgments of them. "After all, any woman can prevent being raped by tightening her vaginal muscles."

The rest of her story and its relevance escaped me as my mind stayed on her last statement. *Wait a minute, lady. You're talking to a rape victim. A rape victim who avoided or escaped penetration beyond the vaginal muscles. Do you know who you're talking to? Do you understand the law the way it was explained to me? Your office is charging this guy with rape, you know. I mean, lady, it is a bit late to tell me how to avoid being raped. I mean,* lady, *preventing penetration only means chances of pregnancy are reduced. Do you think being treated like a fly whose wings are being pulled off by a schoolboy, being smashed into the earth like a filthy cigarette butt, is nothing as long as you tighten your vaginal muscles and prevent penetration? If you're sitting there telling me this shit because you're an expert on rape, you've got a lot to learn. You're a nice person, but you're talking to a rape victim who's trying to get it together for a trial, not hear a number on how to avoid rape!*

I didn't get to ask anymore questions and was anxious to rest my mind at home.

JOURNAL - June 10, Thursday

I'm not sure how it can be explained—why I didn't go to the hospital after the assault. It's not that I have to explain it myself. The prosecution will have to explain but I wish I could know. Burke asked if I wanted to go to the hospital and I said "no." Why did I say "no"? He didn't push it. I didn't see any reason at the time. I was so "cool," even Jon believed I was in control. I was so determined to get the guy. I didn't think about evidence against him. I knew he had done it. Even in talking to Jameson I didn't think about evidence. It was an obvious truth to me. I was the victim of a crime and the assailant was guilty. It didn't occur to me I might have to prove it!

The next afternoon I waited anxiously for Ms. Parrish to call as she had said she would, to report on the results of the preliminary hearing. The office closed at four-thirty and still she hadn't called. At four-thirty-five I finally called her. She was still there.

"Hello, Mrs. Barr. H'ya doing? What can I do for you?"

"The hearing today . . . ?"

"There were no problems with the evidence at the hearing. He is still charged with rape and all the other charges. His bail was reduced to $40,000. He could use personal property for collateral if he has it. He hasn't met the bail yet though. If he chooses trial by judge, the trial will be this summer. If trial by jury, it will be in October. I'll be talking to you a few weeks before the trial."

"When will you know when the trial will be?"

"I'll let you know as soon as I hear."

I still had so many questions and still wanted to go over the whole story. If I waited to talk to someone in October, I might not remember the details that were going through my head as though it had just happened.

"Well, I can see you next Monday at four if you still have questions."

"O.K."

When I hung up, I realized she was allowing me only one half hour. I wasn't sure we were communicating.

JOURNAL - June 10, Thursday

I feel so wound up and wanting to talk but there isn't much to say at this point. Wish rap sessions were tomorrow but I guess I can last till Saturday. There is so much to think about and so much to get straight but it's all confusion. Glad

Nigel is at Mom's, so I have some quiet. I really miss him but it is fun being able to enjoy Colin alone too. Amazing how much more peaceful it is here without Nigel.

Another crisis past and time to settle back to normal again. It was hard to remember where I'd left off.

JOURNAL - June 11, Friday
I'm feeling lost today. It's been two weeks today since this started. Two very intensive weeks, and now with a poof, I'm left hanging to wait for a trial at some unknown date. I don't know what I think about anything. All my doubts and fears have been sorted and tucked away and I'm not quite sure where they all were put. I have no reactions left, on the surface anyway.

Pastor couldn't come today because he has the flu. It doesn't matter much, just glad to know he's aware and cares.

Rap sessions resumed on Saturday, well timed to provide a release for my new turmoil. It was good for me to deal with other people's problems, especially to listen to recent victims. It was good to be reminded that I had learned some things in the last eight months. Each victim had her own unique combination of reactions and experiences, but we had so many feelings in common. It was reassuring to hear from the older victims that they had reacted as intensely as I did, and it was satisfying to be able to turn to more recent victims to say, "Yeah, I felt that way too." It was a reminder of how far I'd come and that the despair and desperation that had been my world did pass. I had survived another two weeks of renewed stress. The future was predictable. Just sit tight and wait for the trial. Sometimes looking back gives the needed reassurance to look ahead.

On Monday I saw Ms. Parrish. We talked for two hours. I gave her a copy of the report I wrote for the police and filled in extra information that might be helpful. I still had unanswered questions.

"Was my physical condition recorded by Officer Burke?"

"Like what?"

"I had burrs all over my clothes. My face was still coated. I had waited till after I saw the police to wash or change. I'd picked that information up somewhere for what to do if attacked. You know, I didn't destroy any evidence."

"Did anyone else see you then? Your husband was there?"

"Yes, but wouldn't it be better to have it from the police?"

"It doesn't matter. If it's in the police report he'll read it, but he can't be expected to remember now if he didn't write it down. Your husband can give a description. If he testifies though, you can't talk to him during the trial. Witnesses aren't allowed to talk to each other."

Can't talk to him? It seemed an impossible rule. It didn't seem worth it, but if there was no testimony of my condition, there would be no evidence at all that it even happened. I was careful not to destroy the evidence until the police came, but I didn't point it out to anyone. I didn't even give him the details that would have made him look for evidence on me. There I sat unwashed for nothing. The police don't go around looking for evidence when they don't even know the crime! How could a case go to court with no evidence that there had even been a crime? No evidence that I was even at the lake?

"Can you tell me what Burke's report says? Does he give any description of me?"

"Sure. We have a copy of his report. It gives the description you gave. You're not getting cold feet, are you? You don't have anything to worry about. That's our job. Listen, I'll be right beside you the whole time. Don't worry about anything. His defense will be misidentification. Are you sure this is the right guy?"

"Oh, yes. I am sure." I never saw the police report.

"Well, his lawyer is still sure he is innocent. He is an old friend of the accused. His family doesn't believe it either. By the way, don't be afraid of Mr. Canfield. He came on strong at the lineup, but he is really very nice. I know him well, and I'm sure he is totally convinced this guy is innocent. Let's go into the courtroom. There's a trial going with Judge Lewis. He is one of two judges who might try your case."

As we walked down the hallway to the old part of the courthouse, she described the setting. "There could be strange people in the courtroom during your trial, going in and out. We don't have too many observers here usually, but sometimes people just come to see a trial. The family will probably be there. They could be emotional or sneer at you or just react in disbelief. Don't let it bother you."

We entered the double doors of the courtroom and sat in the last row. It was Perry Mason's backdrop. High formal ceilings with decorative molding, chandeliers, a large state emblem behind the judge's high bench, tall windows on both sides. There was enough seating for a crowd, but only the bare essentials were in attendance. There was no jury. It was a very quiet scene. An attorney was arguing a point. There was no witness on the stand. The judge looked more asleep than alert. We stayed long enough for my imagination to try to picture the missing parts. I had the setting, the atmosphere, but it was no more real than it had been.

"Yes, it was helpful. Thank you, but do you think you could tell me if there is a rape trial or even a jury trial coming up that I could come in to see?"

"Sure, I'll let you know, but don't get cold feet about this. We're here to protect you. Another trial would be very different from yours. Different attorney, different people, totally different case, you know. He could even plead guilty and that would be it. Don't worry about this trial now, you hear?"

I'd asked all my questions and gotten a lot of information. The total picture of the trial couldn't be supplied until it happened. I'd learned as much as I could.

"I'll let you know as soon as I hear when the trial will be. If you have any questions, be sure to call me."

It was raining when I left and the courthouse was dark and empty. It looked like an ancient institution. With nothing more to think about until the trial, I drove home to normal.

Tuesday night I was reminded again of how unsettled my fears were. Perhaps the coming trial made me more aware of my vulnerability.

JOURNAL - June 15, Tuesday

The air conditioner repairman came this evening. I didn't realize he was coming. I'm sure he said he'd give me a call early this week. He came at about eight. The kids were in bed and I'd been sitting, reading. Jon was at a meeting. Eight is a weird hour for a repairman. I was more than a bit uneasy. The house was closed up to keep it cool. I got Nigel up. I was total ice. He was very talkative and friendly, but I would have preferred that he silently went about his job. He talked to Nigel a lot. I listened to his questions, waiting for an "information type." There weren't any. He broke the gasket so the air conditioner doesn't work at all now. He said he'd come back at 8 A.M. tomorrow to fix it. "Guess you'll just have to open up the house and hope it rains." He seemed overly apologetic, maybe because he sensed my suspicious nature. It's boiling in here, but I'm afraid to open the windows. Wish Jon would get home. This is ridiculous. The repairman said he'd come at eight in the morning to put in the gasket he broke. This is so dumb.

JOURNAL - June 21, Monday

Jon and I have been grumbling at each other a lot. He is depressed and grumbles and I get mad at his grumbling and grumble back. We were up late last night, then I couldn't sleep. I started thinking about the trial, of the assault. I was really tense. Why should anyone believe my story? Why should they believe that I am sure of my identification? What if it's a hung jury? A new trial? Not guilty verdict? How would a jury interpret my story?

JOURNAL - June 23, Wednesday

I have come a long way. A few months ago I worried what I'd wear when the weather got warm. But I'm not even worried about being covered head to toe now. I'm not hiding. Things are better.

I feel like a very changed me. Not just a return to "normal" but a bigger change has begun. I feel more assertive, more active on my own thoughts. I see women so differently and understand their role much better. I understand why women have been expected to be submissive and passive, why they "agreed" to it, how it is perpetuated, what its effects are, and what the obstacles and disadvantages are now in trying to overcome these bonds. I really was not aware of how male dominated our thoughts, and even language, are. With childbirth I certainly became aware of the myths that were obviously perpetuated and created by men who tried to understand, tried to imagine. Through male thinking, childbirth is suffering. Through male thinking, the answer is anesthesia. Our society is totally dominated by the male point of view. I suddenly understand why equality of employment is not just an economic issue. I understand it with blacks and other minorities too. I had only seen it as an economic right of the individual. I had not realized that it was a right, a need, of society.

JOURNAL - June 24, Thursday

Gads, I'm in an explosive mood. I'm not sure what's bugging me. I saw Margot but she didn't find what's bugging me either. We talked about the trial, how I feel about it, but that's not my problem today. When I got home I expected the kids would nap but instead I spent the afternoon cuddling Colin and waiting on Nigel. Jon came home and went downstairs for some quiet while the kids screamed on. When he came up I just yelled and crabbed at him.

That night I went to sleep early to escape the tensions but woke up within an hour in the midst of the terror of the initial shock of my assault. I hadn't felt it since a couple of weeks after the attack. It wouldn't go away. I thrashed stubbornly to dispel the memories. I had a right to be at the lake that day, my mind kept repeating. I had a right to the tranquillity of the woods. But I realized I wasn't picturing the woods where I fell victim, I was picturing the pine woods of Minnesota where I would be the next week. I would be taking the children for three weeks to my family's cabin. Jon could not go, but my mother would be there. I had been looking forward to the trip and was sure I could handle it until my mother's call that night.

"It's so wonderful, the whole family will be at the lake together this year—except Jon. Just think, *all* the grandchildren! Dana just called and said his whole family will be there. And of course Marc and Michelle and your sister."

My tranquil dreams of the lake were shattered.

JOURNAL - June 25, Friday

I go to the lake for peace not a mob scene. I don't even want to go now. I don't have to go all the way to Minnesota to see my family. I don't even want to see them, not for relaxation anyway! I wish Jon could go. How delightful if we could have the lake to ourselves. Maybe he could learn to love the lake too if it wasn't all filled with my relatives. I can't stay there alone though. I wanted to be there when Mom was there. I knew Marc and Michelle would be there but not *everyone*. I really want to go to the lake but not like this. Damn. Wish somehow Jon and I could arrange to go at another time by ourselves but I can't see how we could do it this summer.

During the next week, I resolved I would make the best of the situation at the lake. I loved the lake, I needed the lake, and would concentrate on relaxing there, avoiding my family as much as possible.

The day before leaving, I got a call from Kathy who hadn't called as often as she had before October. I told her that my assailant had been caught.

"Oh, that's good. It's good it's all over. We'll have to get together when you get back from vacation. We'll be going to the mountains for a week too."

I didn't want to force the topic on her, but I was disappointed that she could not acknowledge that part of my life, especially when she had been involved at the beginning. Because we couldn't play tennis that day in October, I had gone for a walk in the woods. She heard about my fate when we had to cancel our weekend baby-sitting offer. I had seen her that weekend. It hurt that she couldn't seem to understand what was dominating my life.

On the morning of my departure for Minnesota, I called Ms. Parrish as I hadn't heard anything from her about the trial date. She had said she would let me know, but she didn't say how much warning she would give me. I would be gone for three weeks and didn't want to come home to a surprise trial.

"So glad you called, Mrs. Barr. Yes, he has decided on a jury trial, so it will be in October."

I guessed that meant he wasn't intending to plead guilty.

CHAPTER IX

As THE small plane descended, the lakes shimmered with the sunlight. Each pine tree curtsied in its own identity, finally escaping the green sea that had hidden it a few thousand feet higher. I watched our own shadow grow as we turned the final approach leg for landing. It was a different world I was entering. Flying provided a magical transformation. A time machine changing everything except the calendar. The lakes and pine trees were the background to a different culture. The people of the lakes held a different relationship to me than those I had left. I wasn't positive I was still me.

I had expected my cousin to meet us, but instead, my aunt and uncle stood in front of the tiny terminal, waving. One embracing hug from my aunt lifted responsibility from my shoulders as my uncle lifted my luggage from my hand. I was aware I was under her care for the rest of my journey and felt a mixture of relief and resentment. I had managed the trip successfully on my own. I wanted to be competent, to show I was competent, but I didn't fight my aunt's desire to take over. I was agreeable to being her ward, at least until we got to the cabin.

Michelle and her household were not due to arrive with my mother at the cabin until the next day, so that night I shared the cabin with my cousins.

"Yes, we have plenty of blankets," I assured her. "No, it's really no problem at all to have Nigel sleep on the floor. He is very used to it and I'm sure the draft won't be a problem."

I was awakened early the next morning by Colin. His sleeping patterns definitely showed that he was Jon's offspring. No one in my family functioned on so little sleep. Though I was glad to be able to watch the mist rise off the lake and to soak up the silence of the early morning, I thought how nice it would be when Mom arrived. She usually was up early and would take care of her grandson so I could sleep in.

I was wide awake and fully functioning for Michelle's midmorning arrival. They had driven all night and everyone, except the kids, was glassy-eyed. "Why don't you guys get some rest and I'll take the kids." My suggestion was appreciated and quickly accepted.

Mom only rested a short time before she was in the kitchen, working on lunch. "Jenn, keep the kids outside so they don't wake Marc and Michelle. Why don't you take them down to the lake and I'll bring sandwiches down for them." I obeyed.

That afternoon was surrendered to a family get-together. Aunts, uncles, and cousins all gathered as a picnic began to form. There were no telephones in the cluster of cabins, so picnics happened more often than they were planned. The lake held its own code of behavior and traditional patterns, which were passed on from one generation to the next. My great-grandparents had homesteaded on that land. When my grandmother inherited it, she lived in town, and part of the land was sold off for summer cabins. A large parcel was later divided among my aunts and uncles as summer cabins. It was a clan complex where gradual changes took place as one generation gave way to the next, but for each generation, the lake represented the childhood which they tried to preserve.

There was a large gathering to welcome the new arrivals. "Look at how Nigel's grown!" "You know I hadn't even seen the baby yet!" "You're so skinny! We've gotta put some weight on you!"

The questions too often ended with "And what have *you* been doing this year?"

"Oh, some needlepoint . . . and uh, we went to California in May." I ended the sentence hurriedly, relieved that I'd found something significant to say. I considered responding casually, "I've been bordering on insanity on and off because of the rape, you know, but other than that everything is fine." But they would have smiled at the witty reply.

No one brought up the topic of what had really been occupying me during the last year. It was not a topic for a social occasion, but I would have felt more comfortable if someone had acknowledged the fact.

It took half a picnic before I began to ache for solitude. I edged myself to the dock where I could sit quietly with Nigel and discuss the ducks. I waited for the volley of smiles to settle down to quieter visits. I looked forward to quiet times with Michelle. We'd be together for over a week; we would finally have a chance to really talk.

During the week Michelle and I spent a lot of time talking, in bits and snatches. We weren't alone often. The distance between us and our children was never very large. Mom or Marc often dropped in on our conversations as they passed by, though Marc rarely dwelled long on our concerns. His purpose in the interruptions was either a friendly word as he took a break from his book or a suggestion that we all go for a walk or swim. Mom's interruptions, casual or sustained, guaranteed a change in subject matter.

However, one evening Mom was out visiting, Marc was in a corner reading, and the kids were all asleep. Our conversation began on the subject of criminal justice and led to current politics. Mom entered as Jimmy Carter's presidential candidacy came into our talk. I was glad we'd passed from justice.

"What do you know about him, Michelle?" I asked.

"Well, he's got a nice smile, but I'm not sure how he stands on a lot of issues."

"Do you trust him?" I asked, pushing for a firmer opinion.

Mom sighed. "Why don't we play some rummy?"

"Thanks, Mom, but there're only three of us to play." I

turned back to Michelle. "Do you think Carter would be good for ecology?"

"Oh, Jenn, we're at the lake. Let's not talk about politics," Mom interjected. I felt momentary shame that I was pushing a topic no one else was interested in but caught myself this time, realizing Mom was the only one who *wasn't* interested in the topic.

"Mom, if you don't want to discuss the election you don't have to, but Michelle and I were having a good talk."

"Well, the election isn't till November. You have plenty of time to discuss it. Now how about some Yahtzee?" Mom stated with her congenial smile.

"No thanks. Not tonight." And I got up to get Michelle and me more coffee.

Michelle had gotten up and was looking down to the lake during my exchange with Mom. "The lake looks so smooth. Let's go down by the lake if the mosquitoes aren't too bad." She wasn't addressing anyone in particular when she spoke, but she glanced at me for a response.

"Sure," I said. "Want to come, Marc?"

"Uh . . . oh, I'll come down in a minute."

We carried our cups down with us, not talking until we reached the dock.

"She's really beginning to bug me," Michelle said.

"Mom?"

"Yeah. She's really been different while we've been here."

"Different?"

"I couldn't believe how well you just handled her. I felt as if she totally closed the subject because she likes Ford. She didn't want to hear, therefore we were supposed to stop talking. But you were so cool. You hardly even noticed. You just let her know she wasn't going to win and I think you totally devastated her. No one else in the family could have done that."

I was cool? I was seething! I had been very impatient with Mom since she had come. I had expected more help with the kids from her, and she had shown no interest in them. I had expected more comfort from her in my anxieties since Jon was not there. I tucked away my hurt feelings by reminding myself I wasn't Mama's little girl. I had my own family.

These stifled feelings surfaced as Michelle spoke, and I realized that it wasn't just rejection that made me impatient with her. While she was refusing the role of the Protective Mother, she still wanted the control of a Manipulative Mother. She constantly corrected and directed us in meaningless ways. "Don't use those plates, use these." "Whose going to wash the dishes tonight?" "Why are you putting the ice in the lemonade now?" It was like none of us could possibly make a decision on which plates to use or remember that dishes had to be washed after we ate. She treated us like irresponsible teenagers, and I was reacting like a rebellious teenager in return.

"Yeah, Michelle. I see what you mean. I thought it was just me. The other day when Mrs. Warner invited us all over for coffee? I figured I'd go over when the kids woke up from their naps. Mom said I was being selfish and couldn't lead my life being so antisocial. I had a responsibility and on and on. She expected me to either wake the kids up or to leave them sleeping alone in the cabin. I mean I don't know if Mrs. Warner even remembers me or knows I'm here. How could I hurt her feelings? But I ended up feeling guilty no matter how hard I defended myself. I guess when I've lived with it all my life, it's hard for me to see the problem like you. I've just been irritated and impatient and feeling guilty about the way I've been treating Mom."

"Well I've been exploding since the day we got here. Like suddenly I'm intruding on her turf and only she knows how anything should be done. It's been a horrible vacation and Marc just keeps telling me I'm too sensitive, too critical. He doesn't see it at all."

We had spent a lot of time talking, but it had taken us five days to share our current feelings. The rest of the stay at the lake was much easier. I stood up to Mom more frequently and stopped feeling guilty about it. I became aware of how this subtle trait of hers affected my self-confidence. She made me feel inadequate, awkward, and guilty. She had never allowed me to develop my confidence because she never allowed me to trust my own judgment. She used guilt instead of a hickory stick to keep me in line.

Leaving the lake was not as difficult as it usually was. The lake had not provided the peaceful rejuvenation of the soul that its magic usually brought, but the discomfort caused by that disappointment had given birth to a new dimension which would provide strength for me later when I needed it. Because Mom had pushed me where I was tender, I finally became rebellious to her methods and values. It was a stage of development I had missed as a teenager. I had been obedient and painfully aware of my responsibilities to image. I had snobbishly looked down on those my age who were experimenting with who they were. I knew who I was, who I had to be. I was what my mother wished me to be.

At the lake that summer I painfully turned around and said to my mother, "I don't care what you think of me. This is the way I must do things. This is the way I am. I'm sorry if it doesn't make you happy, I'm not deliberately trying to hurt you. You will have to deal with your hurt your way as you have left me to deal with mine my way. And this, Mom, is my way." It wasn't learned suddenly at the lake, nor was it learned completely there, but my mother's heavy influence was what I had to break through before I could change.

It felt good to be home again. I had missed Jon terribly. With him I wasn't alone anymore. I wasn't solely responsible for my children or solely enraptured by their special activities. I had someone to share my thoughts and feelings with. Before these attributes of marriage were dulled by the expectations of them which time brings, I felt newly in love and very content.

I was motivated to get my house in order, literally. During this respite from turmoil and confusion, I was grateful for the relief from pressure that the middle of the summer provides. It was easy to hide and let everyone assume we were off on vacation. I was content in my world of Jon, children, and house.

I was ready for Karen's call when she informed me that the next training session for the Rape Crisis Center was coming up. It was scheduled for early August. It seemed that it was ordained for me to have missed the last training in May, considering what lay between the two sessions. I felt stable enough now to do the job right.

An orientation meeting was held a few days before the

all-day training workshop. About ten women were there and we each introduced ourselves and stated why we wanted to join the Center. As the introductions went around the circle, I felt a mounting anxiety. I had rehearsed what I would say —a few words on how valuable the Center's work was and how meaningful it was to victims and how much I wanted to be a part of it and ending quietly with the fact that I knew its worth because I was a victim. I tried to listen intently to each introduction, but their words faded as they approached. I glanced at Karen as my turn came, then dropped my eyes to her feet. "I'm Jennifer Barr and I was a victim." My face burned. The next person graciously picked up quickly on her introduction. I was furious at myself for having failed. *I'm not ashamed, dammit, so why am I so embarrassed!*

The discussion of the Center's work was painful in itself. I knew most of the information through experience or from the rap sessions, but the discomfort came when they discussed the feelings and reactions of victims. I was being drawn back into the victim identification; I was being painfully reminded of how tender my feelings still were on the subject. I wanted to speak out for victims, but I was there as a counselor-trainee, not a victim.

In the days before the training I talked to Karen about my doubts that I was up to it. She reassured me that I was. "If you're not, you can find out on Saturday. Go through the training, then decide."

I phoned Margot about my doubts, and she too urged me to get into counseling. "It'll be so good for you to be able to help other victims, and I know you'll be a tremendous help to them."

I did want to get into the Center. I had been so disappointed in May when I missed training then. Now I was getting cold feet. The more I tried to read the Handbook and prepare myself for Saturday, the more flashbacks and thoughts of the approaching trial gripped me. I decided it was probably more fear of the training itself that was frightening me and I'd feel O.K. after the training session. After all, I could survive one uncomfortable day in order to pursue my goal of doing something about rape and to help other victims.

Saturday's training went as expected, painful and exhausting. I had been very nervous and I wasn't sure I'd even be accepted as a counselor, considering my emotional state that day. Karen called me on Sunday to give me the verdict. "You were accepted unprovisionally. You did fine. Now stop worrying about it." O.K. they judged me stable, I'll trust their judgment.

The next Thursday I got my court summons. Delivered by the deputy sheriff. ". . . the following named witnesses to testify for the State in the above entitled case and the same returnable on Wednesday and Thursday the 27th and 28th day of October, 1976, at 9:45 o'clock A.M." My name was the first listed, then two other women, followed by Detective Jameson. It was very official. I noticed that Officer Burke was not on the summons.

The summons wasn't a surprise, but I didn't expect it so soon. It was the middle of August. I had two months to wait. My initial curiosity about the summons turned into questions about it. I shrugged my shoulders and tucked the paper away. "Now I know the date anyway. Maybe my life can be more settled. At least something to plan around."

That evening I received a call from one of the other women listed on the summons.

"I got this summons today and your name is listed on it too. Do you know what it's about?"

I hesitated in answering her. How much discussion is allowed between witnesses? The law is so funny, what if we said more than we're supposed to? Do I let on that I know who she is by referring to the incident and the date? Do I tell her why I was summoned and let her figure out herself how she is involved? I had no training for the witness role. What were the rules for this game?

"Uh . . . well . . . you know the lineup you went to in June. . . . You were there weren't you?" I was sure she was the teenager there. She couldn't have forgotten. I had been spending half my time since then with little else on my mind, and she didn't even know what the summons was for. She did remember the lineup and thanked me.

That night the questions began to turn to doubts. Why was that girl being summoned when she hadn't identified anyone at the lineup? Hadn't Ms. Parrish talked to her at all since the lineup? I had been told her case was being dropped. Had my question on that matter just been misunderstood? Why wasn't Burke on the summons? He certainly seemed pertinent to the case. I began to doubt things Ms. Parrish had told me. I wasn't sure we had been communicating on the same level. Jon didn't seem to think these details were anything to worry about. He was right, of course. I'd find out the details soon enough. There was no need to dwell on these doubts. Yet I did. I lay awake that night in torment.

I went over what I could remember from my discussions with Ms. Parrish. The other women hadn't identified him, at least not positively. Mine was the strongest case against him because of both the positive identification and the most serious charges, but the police were sure all the lake cases were related. I would have felt better if I weren't going to be the only witness. But if they weren't even having Burke testify, what support would I have in my testimony? I tried to chase all these thoughts of the trial out of my head. I had more than two months to learn the answers to my questions. In my readings for rape counseling, I had just read the chapter on the courts. I was beginning to feel a reality about the process which I couldn't fit into the life I knew.

JOURNAL - August 10, Tuesday
I've been getting stuff done but at the same time it seems so pointless. I feel like I'm living in an ideal world—a good husband, beautiful kids, friends, money—yet I'm blowing it all. Jon and I are always bickering; I can't seem to do anything right for him. I just yell at the kids so much. I can see them getting tenser.

"I don't see why you have to worry about those details now." Jon's words rang in my head. He was right. It wasn't the details I was worried about. It was me. I wished I could stop feeling, stop thinking, because my thoughts kept circling around to the most frightening unknown. Was I worth all the trouble? Did this drama have any real value? Did I have any real value? I wanted to know how I fit into the order of the universe but the order that I believed in was being destroyed around me.

JOURNAL - August 19, Thursday

I feel like I'll be a victim for the rest of my life. I'm obsessed by rape and yet I want to forget it and be "normal." Why can't I just go back to my dreams of gardening and weaving! Why can't I just forget it! Everything seems so trivial and meaningless. The worthwhile things I'm ruining—the kids, Jon. I'm destroying everything around me. I just want to love Jon and love my Nigel and Colin and make their worlds beautiful. That is the first priority, the only meaning. But all I do is scream and bitch and reject them. Why am I living like this?

During a visit with Bart and Sarah, the conversation turned to the subject of rape. Sarah asked if anything was new with my case. Jon and Bart were on the couch across the room from us, discussing the Nobel Prize or Indian artifacts, and seemed a world away from us as we spoke quietly. Sarah was curious about the legal procedures, so I shared what I knew. The conversation on the couch paused and I was aware that Bart was listening to us. He had his own questions on the topic and joined the discussion. I had been reading a lot, I had had my rape-counseling training. I had information I could share and I needed their perspective on the topic. I felt reassured that even Bart was interested in the topic I was so concerned about.

Jon had gone to the kitchen to get a Coke and sat quietly drinking it. He disappeared again into the library, returning with a book he asked to borrow and announced we should get home.

"But it's just a little after eleven," I protested.

"Yeah, but I'm the one that is going to be awakened at

seven by the kids that you never seem to hear on Saturday mornings."

I understood by his tone that he was irritated, so I followed.

We didn't speak as we drove through the heavy traffic. By the time we got on the open road I was impatient with him.

"Well, are you going to tell me what's the matter?"

"Nothing. I'm just tired."

Dammit. There he goes again. Nothing, huh? I waited for him to change his mind and tell me.

"You're smoking too much again, Jenn," he said quietly, casting an unfriendly glance at me.

"Is that the only reason you're mad at me? I can see you're mad. Why did you want to leave?"

"I'm just sick of rape. That's all you ever talk about. It's the same stuff over and over, and I don't want to have to sit and listen to it all night. You never talk about anything else. I'm sick of it!"

You're sick of it! You're sick of it! He could have been telling me he was leaving me, and I wouldn't have felt more deserted. There were no more words. There were no tears. I had been entombed.

That weekend I engrossed myself in quiet projects. I picked up unfinished projects, carefully chosen ones. The reasons for the choices were not immediately obvious, but they were projects that I knew only I could do and that were important to me. I began with organizing the file on family history that I had collected through the years. I worked on some weaving that had been sitting on the loom. I avoided Jon and the children.

On Tuesday Karen called to ask if she should pick me up for the Crisis Center meeting that night.

"Karen, I can't do it."

"Of course you can. You're just a little nervous about it. Everyone is at first."

"No, Karen, I can't."

We talked a long time about the Center, about counselors, about fears. "Well, Jenn, listen. Don't make a firm decision yet. See how you feel after the meeting. I'll be sure to be available whenever you are on phone duty, so that if you get a case, just call me."

She didn't allow me to get out of it. She did make sense. I was just nervous. I was just afraid of the unknown.

JOURNAL - August 24, Tuesday

I've been so anxious to become involved with the Crisis Center and now I can't make it. Tonight was the first meeting. Counselors talking about their cases and I tried to imagine me dealing with the situations. I was swallowing tears just hearing their stories. I can't do it. I'm feeling so freaky. So isolated. It's just as well that no one knows when they can't do anything anyway. Everyone's just tired of hearing about it. I'm tired of hearing about it. I should really put all my rape books away and not even think about the subject. I want to scream. Run screaming through the woods till I drop. I don't want autumn to come. Maybe it'll rain the whole colorful time. I hope it turns freezing in the middle of September. No blue skies, no gold leaves. Go away all of you. Go away everything. Let me sit and stare at the tube that we can't even get ETV on. Let me just sit till it's all gone.

JOURNAL - August 25, Wednesday

Maybe I don't want to get rid of my rape victim status. Maybe that is my problem. It is my area of expertise. I am special. I am unique. What was I before? How can I cling to it and scream that it's not going away at the same time? I'm so tired of it all. I want to scream when someone says, "Considering all you've been through, it's no wonder you feel the way you do." Don't pity me. You don't know what I feel at all. My situation has nothing to do with anything! Only I am allowed to use it as an excuse so I don't have to explain.

I get so upset about everyone's problems. I shouldn't even listen to the news. "Man Mugged" because he stepped in a puddle. "Five Teenagers Killed in Car Crash." This is local, right here in River City. Thugs, hoodlums, death, tears. But it's reality. We've gotta live with it. It could be starvation or war. Why am I so obsessed with violence and sadness? It's all so senseless.

On Thursday Jon forgot his lunch and called to ask me to bring it to him. It was a crisp, cool day for August. I gathered the kids with no resentment for the effort he had asked me to put into bringing his lunch. He never seemed to realize that what might normally be a twenty-minute excursion would take an hour with two small children. I left his lunch at the receptionist's desk because she couldn't locate him immediately. I didn't want to wait. I wanted to get home out of the sunshine as soon as possible. The kids were quiet in the back seat as I approached the turn that brought the road parallel to the river. The river was directly ahead of me, with the sun shining through the trees and shimmering on the water. In backwater areas the images of the trees and the pure blue sky flickered, beckoning me. It would be so easy. I was hypnotized by the song of the waters that called me to become part of the river that flowed gently past the world. The sound of tires crunching gravel beside the road abruptly interrupted the water's song. I had forgotten the part of me that carried my dreams, the part of me that sat silently in the back seat, trusting me.

"Why did we stop, Mama?"

"I don't know, Nigel. . . . I'm not sure." But tears clouded my eyes as I realized that I wasn't even upset about what I had almost done.

I made an appointment to see Margot, hoping she could tell me why I shouldn't lie down deep in the woods and quit, hoping she could make me believe there were open meadows ahead, that someone was searching for me and I would be found. She wasn't as helpful as usual. I wasn't helpful.

"But, Margot, nothing matters. . . ."

"Oh, Jennifer, you know things matter. Don't tell me Jon and your children don't mean anything to you. That's just a crazy thing to say, Jennifer."

I know, I know. I won't try your patience with that anymore. It was silly of me to try to explain. I crossed my legs and sat back in my chair.

"Actually, Margot, my problem is that I'm not ready to do rape counseling."

"You have so much to offer other victims, Jennifer. You'd be such an asset to the Center, you know. You have to try to stop thinking of yourself as a victim. You have to close that chapter of your life." She gave me time between each sentence to understand what she was saying. I was trying to believe her. "I really believe it is a decision you can make, that you need to make. Think about what is important to you and channel your thoughts in that direction. There is so much more to you than just being a rape victim, but you're letting it control your life."

"But the trial . . ."

"Go and talk to the State's attorney to get your questions answered if that will help, but, Jennifer, the trial isn't until October."

"But the Crisis Center—I don't think I should do it now." Because I couldn't confess my deepest fears, I pressed her for help with my tangible dilemmas.

"Of course you should. You have to prove to yourself you can take it. I know you can. You need the sense of helping others. You could be such a big help to someone else."

She was turning me around in circles because our minds were thinking in opposing directions. *I don't know what you're even saying because it doesn't matter what you're saying.* She wouldn't have accepted that either. It didn't leave her any place to start.

"Look at your future. What do you expect of life? In ten years? In thirty years? What dreams do you have? Think about it this week and we'll make an appointment for next week."

Fine, fine. But I see no future. The past wasn't bad, equal elations and difficulties, but it doesn't exist anymore. The present continues. Nothing wrong. The future isn't there. It doesn't matter. It isn't there.

I had a dwindling pile of unfinished projects at home, but I had one big project that I knew I had to finish. My needlepoint picture for Nigel had been set aside again in the spring. Now it occupied all of my time. It filled time, it bought time. I knew I had to finish it for Nigel. I thought of death often. I argued with myself about it. I consoled myself with it because it was the only escape I had from my mind. There was nothing to save. Only a needlepoint to finish and then nothing. I could see no reason for my existence.

At church on Sunday, I didn't pray. I watched people, wondering why they bothered. If they heard the answers to their prayers they'd wish they hadn't asked. The sermon's words began to penetrate. "They torture themselves with despair because they are immature or selfish instead of turning to Jesus who provides paradise on earth." A spark crackled in me. *Sure, opium and liquor work the same way.*

That afternoon Marc and Michelle visited. We chatted. I hid my depression, but Michelle talked about a depressed friend of hers. "Depression is caused by selfishness. I don't mean when there is a good reason to be depressed like you have. Just people who get hung up on it and are depressed without reason. Just 'cause they aren't happy with themselves they think they have problems worse than other people. There are always worse situations to think about. Nothing is too desperate not to see the good side. If they'd get out and help people who really need help, they'd be fine but they get depressed thinking of themselves all the time."

No, Michelle, you don't understand. There is a point of depression when nothing matters. The only unhappiness is self-discontent and the situation doesn't matter. When a person is happy about a little item, we don't ask why they are excited about such a little thing. We don't say, "How can you be happy when you have so little?" That would be ab-

surd because it is not to be compared. If one loves life and loves oneself, nothing is depressing. It is only sad. Depression is doubt. Doubt of values, doubt of self, doubt of truth, doubt of meaning. It doesn't matter. Nothing matters.

It wouldn't do any good to try to tell her. I didn't want to discuss it. I wanted everyone to just leave me alone. I didn't want any advice, it was all empty words. I was tired of trying. Why did everyone else seem to think they had the answer? Did they know something I didn't? I didn't *want* to die. I didn't want to miss anything in case a good experience might come along. Everyone else can hang in there. I knew I could do it as well as anyone. If I could just hang on, maybe I'd learn. I needed to be on the dock at the lake, considering all this. I knew things would make more sense there. Things did.

JOURNAL - August 29, Sunday

I need to do more things with the kids. I need to be away from suburbia. It's stifling. Where is my room to breathe and think? A place for the kids and me to wander, explore, learn together about life. I've become too suburban. I'm afraid of loneliness. What should it matter? No one was around when I needed them last October in the middle of suburbia. No one hears the screams, the sobbing. There is too much noise, too much screaming and sobbing, and everyone becomes deaf. Others function. Do they just have a greater tolerance for the noise? No, this isn't my dream. I've forgotten my dreams. I don't hear the leaves or the waves anymore. It is so quiet on Aunt Esther's dock.

The gut instinct for survival had returned. I had no more reason for wanting to live than I had had before, but it took more energy than I had to die. So I went on to the next day, as people do.

Because I had an appointment with Margot the next week, I went. Last week's questions were still pending. I didn't want to have to say, "No, Margot, I couldn't think of any dreams." But she didn't ask. She was off into questions on values and reality.

"Wait, Margot, I'm not there yet. Let's start with why I'm still alive." She couldn't probe something so obvious.

"Jennifer, I can't help you unless you can talk about what's bothering you."

Nothing's bothering me, don't you see, Margot? It doesn't matter and if nothing matters it can't bother either. No, you don't see, do you? It's that sometimes values aren't valuable and reality isn't real and it doesn't matter.

"But you can't just go off to your room and hide anymore." She had been accustomed to my struggles but this time I wasn't struggling. "You're grown-up now, and don't you shrug your shoulders at me again."

I shrugged my shoulders. *Now, now, Margot. Let's go back to the beginning. I'm alive and how I manage to be alive is not important. It's just survival that I'm interested in. I survived even when I stopped trying to survive. I'd like for you just to understand. There is nothing to talk about if you don't.*

She sensed that I was escaping as I stared out the window.

"Jennifer, are you listening to me? If it's the trial that's bothering you, talk to the State's attorney. He's the only one that can answer your questions about it. Be a little assertive. Don't wait for them to call you."

Assertive? I'm not listening to you. I think you said

"trial." *It's only going to happen, I'm not going to do it. Jennifer Barr is not going through a trial.* I didn't hear her, but my knees made my stomach churn. "Say the magic word and you win the Triple Clown." I grinned and shrugged my shoulders.

She thought I sounded very confused and wanted to see me the next week. Perhaps in a week I'd be ready to talk about reality and values.

I did work on it that week. I said "trial" over and over and sometimes I listened to the word. I just wanted it to be over with, I didn't want to think about it.

JOURNAL - September 2, Thursday

And God said, "Jennifer, here is your challenge. I'm making it tough, I'm giving you everything you need. No limitations. To make it tougher I've given you a thinking mind. Every once in a while I choose someone for the Ultimate Challenge (to live after releasing life as pointless). There are no boundaries, no rules, unless you set them up. You can run as far and as fast as you like. There are no markers to tell you how far or in what direction you go. You've got the chance and the challenge for discovery. It's now."

"But what's there to be discovered? What am I looking for? Why are you picking on me? Everyone will think I'm crazy if I don't go by the rules."

"You won't know till you try it. You can't fail because there's no failing mark. It is your choice. You can build fences if you want, like everyone else. It is your choice."

Jon and I took a trip to New England to get away and relax together. Autumn was blooming there under blue skies. We took walks in the mountains and rape was behind every tree. I hid my flashbacks from Jon and didn't sleep at night. We came home to reminders of reality, and I started taking Valium. "Yes, we had a beautiful trip to New England, the weather was perfect." I didn't try to explain.

JOURNAL - September 25, Saturday
I bought The Perfect Bowl at a craft fair today. I just hold it and it is magic. I think there are some dreams inside. If I love and dream, I can endure.

CHAPTER X

I DON'T know how long the phone rang before it finally
woke me. It was 5 A.M. on a Sunday morning. Karen was on
counselor duty that night and had been called on a rape
case. She was asking me if I wanted to go with her on this
case. My mind fought to go back to sleep, but there was a
force inside me that wouldn't let me. I had to go. I got up
and dressed quickly. The roads were very quiet at that time
of the week, and the fog that wisped across the road added
to the surrealism of the trip. I munched a Granola Bar on the
way and wished I'd remembered to brush my teeth. My
tongue was dry as I tried to picture the victim I would meet
at the hospital. Who was she? How was she taking it?

Fortunately, I was not the official counselor as I arrived
rather late on the scene. The woman, a plain thirty-five-

year-old, had already been examined, and Karen was in the examining room trying to work out some difficulties with her. I introduced myself to the nurse on duty, and she explained what was happening. The woman only wanted to press charges for the robbery but not the rape. She had a lot of other problems she was dealing with—a recent separation from her husband, conflicts with her mother whom she was living with. She was afraid they'd find out if the rape were reported. She wasn't sure she wanted to talk to the officer at all. The police officer was waiting patiently in the hall for things to be resolved. He was relying heavily on Karen as a communication link between them and seemed very understanding of the situation. Karen went back and forth between the hall and the examining room until the victim emerged. The victim was hostile to the officer and suspicious of everyone else.

"Why should anyone care anyway?"

I stood back and watched helplessly. I wanted to grab her and scream with her. "I don't know why anyone should care. No one does care, really. Not the way you care." But I cared.

She finally, reluctantly, went with the officer to the police station. It was not the end of the ordeal for her, but Karen and I sat down for some coffee and talk.

"How do you feel now, Jenn?"

"Tired. You did a fantastic job. It was good to see how the officer trusted you, relied on you. It's so good to have their support, but it's a bit scary to know that they have that much faith in us as counselors. You know what I mean?"

"A lot have learned to trust us. It's been a slow process and we still come across skeptics or antagonistic officers, but most of them are glad to have someone else there who has specific training in working with rape victims. We've got a pretty good relationship with the police now. They don't expect perfection from us, but they know we're there to help. How did you feel during it all?"

"Pretty helpless. It was good to get the feel of the hospital atmosphere and all that and I'm sure I learned something, watching you, but I don't know if I could do it. I mean, I know I couldn't have done it like you did."

"Sure you could. With a little experience you'll relax about it. What would you have done if you were on this case alone?"

"Cried. I know I would have just stood there and cried."

"And after you cried, then what would you do?"

"Oh, Karen." I laughed. "You just won't let me get out easily will you?"

"I'm serious. I know you would have been upset. That's why I've said I'd go with you if you got a case. That's why I called you to come tonight. Now that you've been here and been upset and you didn't cry, how do you feel about counseling?"

"I guess you're right. I didn't cry, but I couldn't have said anything. I just stood there. I was thinking of responses to things said, though. Trying to think if I were the counselor and functioning, what I might have said. Your replies were always much better . . . but I was thinking. I may make it yet; give me another ten practice runs and I might be up to a solo . . . maybe."

"Another ten runs, huh? Sorry, sister, we only have so much patience at the Center, but I suspect you could even go it alone if necessary now. You gonna stick with the Center now? Now that you've seen you didn't even cry on your first case?"

"Yeah, yeah, I think there's hope. But, Karen, I am not ready for a solo yet. Stick by me till I get through my first case anyway."

"Sure, Jennifer, you know I'm willing to do that."

I was still shaky as I drove home in the morning twilight, but I had gained enough confidence that morning to convince me to continue working with the Center.

The case experience had come during a transition time, and it influenced the direction I would turn. My depression had bottomed out, and I had begun to look for activities for this life I was enduring. Being alive meant movement and if I stopped going down, I had to go up. I carefully chose activities I could handle. Math was important. As long as I had enrolled in Precalculus, I would drift with the current rather than get out of the water. I committed more time to the Center, to prepare myself for that first solo case. I chose a few concerns, impersonal concerns, to channel my commitment.

I couldn't explain to Jon why my outside interests were so important because I hadn't shared with him the thoughts that had preceded them. I knew he would be upset if he knew any of my midnight thoughts, but he was losing his patience with me. "What am I working myself to death for and then come home to screaming kids and no supper?" His pressures at work didn't help his patience with me. Trying to explain or defend myself only led to added friction between us. I wasn't ready to confess how desperate I had been. He wouldn't have understood why I needed to just fill time.

Not only did Jon have his own problems at work and have to deal with mine at home, he suffered a triple whammie. He had no outlet for his frustrations, no sympathetic ear. While I felt sorry for myself that everyone was forgetting me, people weren't forgetting Jon; they had never remembered him. When I had been painfully in the limelight, he was painfully in my shadow. For the past year my world had revolved around him, clinging to him, dependent on him, he was my ship's anchor. When things were calm, I didn't want the boat to rock unnecessarily by dragging up the anchor. I needed to know he was there, but it was a one-way pull. During more stable times I tried to be sensitive to his needs, but I still wasn't up to handling his demands. I handled the marital tension the way I was handling the trial —I was aware of its existence. It drove me deeper into studying math and devoting energies to the Crisis Center.

JOURNAL - September 28, Wednesday

I'm so frustrated. Jon says it's his situation not his attitude, but it's never the situation. It's not being able to cope with the situation. People survive horrible situations if they have the right attitude. Oh, listen to me talk. Well, I know I'm my own problem. My situation is not impossible. I'm just not prepared for my situation. Oh, damn the world. This is really a stupid way to waste my life. And I knitted little Joel's sweater too small. Damn.

On the last day of September I got a call from Claire, a victim who attended the last rap group.

"Jennifer, I'm really sorry I haven't called you. I know you were interested in coming to my trial if mine came up before yours, and I've been meaning to call but things have been a bit confused. The trial has been going on for two days now. I think, I hope, tomorrow will be the last day. I'd like for you to come if you can. . . . Maybe it will help you. But don't feel like you have to."

I had forgotten her promise. I'd forgotten Claire was in the same situation. I couldn't make a committment to go until I had had time to think about it. "I'll try. I really want to. Thanks for calling and keep in touch."

Heavy rain, heavy traffic, and uncertain directions to the courthouse had overtones of a nightmare, the impossible-effort type. Claire wasn't at the courtroom when I arrived, and I realized I didn't know the name of her case or the name of her attorney. There was no way I could find the trial if I had the wrong courtroom. I finally went up to a group of men who looked like lawyers and asked if any of them were representing Claire. With luck one was, but he didn't know where she was. At least it was the right place. Finally Claire arrived, soaked and upset. A friend had said she would drive in with her that morning but had called at the last minute to say she couldn't go because she "didn't have anything to wear." Claire felt understandably frazzled.

Already tense from waiting, I didn't feel that I would be of much help to her. The counseling skills I had been taught were drowned in my emotions. I sat holding Claire's hand and watching her for any sign of how I could help her. The hallway where we waited was filled with people, waiting, talking, coming and going.

The trial was late starting, waiting for the jury to arrive.

Claire had already testified and was sequestered in a dreary jury room, alone, when the trial resumed. I was torn between wanting to be with her and wanting to witness the trial. She made my decision easier by asking me to listen to the testimony so that I could tell her later what was said.

Since I had missed most of the prosecution's testimony, it was hard to follow the defense's case. A drawing easel was heavily used to show floor plans of the room, a map of the car route, details that were discussed over and over with each witness. There was a lot of acting out of exactly how someone was standing, walking, or sitting. A simple statement about place or posture never got past the defense lawyer. The judge didn't seem to be taking his stately position very seriously. When he was required to make a decision, he usually ended it with a flippant remark meant to be funny. I suppose faced with grim trials every day, one has to be somewhat callous and try to keep a sense of humor, but when I knew a person involved, the humor had a cutting edge. The jury was even more depressing to contemplate. They talked among themselves, yawned, stared out the window. Two rows of blank faces. No sign of anything. How aware were they of the proceedings? How many myths floated through their heads? How sincere or responsible were they? How prejudiced? No signs.

I stayed through the closing arguments. The judge instructed the jury about the verdict. He gave the definitions of the charges again and cautioned the jury to remember that the state had to prove its case beyond a reasonable doubt, especially considering "how easy it is for a woman to cry rape"!!! My composure dropped out of my mouth like false teeth. I gripped the pew in front of me to hold myself down. The judge said that! The impartial judge, the blind justice system! Easy!? I was ready to shout at them all what a woman had to endure to press charges. If he had made such a prejudiced statement against the defendant, it would certainly be grounds for a mistrial. Could he possibly legally say such a thing? But the State's attorney's face didn't even flicker. He stood to summarize his case.

The State's closing statement was brief and not persuasive, it was merely an "obvious case of rape." I was prepared for a tedious defense. To be sure he would distort and confuse but even with those thoughts I found it hard to believe anyone smart enough to get through law school would expect anyone to accept that "it was an obvious attempt by a middle-class suburban white girl to cover up her involvement with a black." What a clever cover-up! She called her father and the police immediately after the event, a strange way to hide something. She had to go over every detail of it in court in front of her family, friends, and the general public. Such a simple everyday cover-up! The defense was playing so hard on the stereotypes and prejudices that it seemed it would be obvious and insulting to anyone.

The State's rebuttal was much stronger than the original summary. He tried to dispel the racial issues raised by the defense to the mostly black jury. He never dealt with the question of why any sane woman would falsely "cry rape" or how difficult it would be to carry a lie through months of investigation and raised eyebrows from police and attorneys who don't like to waste time on unprosecutable cases.

I couldn't stay to wait for the verdict. Claire had already left when it was obvious she would not be recalled. I got home late, tense and exhausted. I had witnessed the reality of a trial and needed time to let it soak in. I didn't have the time; the next morning Jon and I were leaving for a four-hour drive to a wedding in Jon's family.

Most of the people at the wedding were from Jon's hometown. I only knew them through Christmas cards or family newsletters so I was content to be an observer while Jon did the visiting. It was an interlude in a foreign society. The people seemed to have stopped growing and had begun aging before they turned twenty. There was a hollowness in their voices that could only be disguised by alcohol. It was hard to imagine Jon growing up with these people. Had he always been different or was the difference established when he left the town? My admiration for Jon grew as I watched and listened to him. If he was aware of the difference, he accepted it without judgment.

The drive home that day was worth many hours of therapy. We talked and, more important, we listened. The kids had been left at home, no interruptions, no distractions. In the car, with a distance of more than two weeks past, I cautiously disclosed the depth of my depression, assuring him I never contemplated suicide.

"God, Jenn. I had no idea. Why didn't you tell me?" *That's just it, Jon, I couldn't.* We returned to each other at a crucial time, and together we thought about the coming trial.

"The problem with today's world," I found myself saying, "is that we treat crises as abnormal, therefore when crisis strikes, the victims are treated as, and react to, being abnormal. Crises are not a requirement of life, but no one is above them. I mean, every day there are thousands of people involved in trials and that is just one crisis. We should treat crises as normal."

I was thankful that I had been able to go to Claire's trial. It gave a reality to trials. They did happen. I didn't like what I saw, but I had an idea of what I was trying to deal with. Her case was very different from what I would face. But there was the framework of reality within which I could think.

I had seen many people, in and out of the courtroom that day, being affected strongly by the process, each coping in his own way. I overheard the conversation of a couple waiting in the hallway.

"Will they sentence you today?"

"No, but I shouldn't get more than a year this time."

"Oh, do you think so? That would be good."

They were discussing a year of their lives the way I'd talk about an hour's nap. They obviously viewed life very differently than I did.

It seemed that ideals and human sensitivity had no place in the courtroom. The lawyers were playing with words and manipulating logic. I found myself chuckling at their antics but refused to relate it to my situation. I had only seen part of one trial, I shouldn't draw conclusions from that. But even in the confusion and disillusionment, there was a calming effect on me. The system was absurd; why should I take it all so seriously?

On Monday I learned Claire's verdict: Acquittal. The taste of disillusionment had prepared me for the verdict, but I was angry and disappointed with the system that allowed it. I didn't wait any longer to get in touch with my State's attorney's office.

"Hello, Ms. Parrish? Jennifer Barr."

"Oh yes, Mrs. Barr. How are you? I've been waiting to hear from you."

Waiting, huh? Did you ever think of calling yourself? No, of course not. It seemed to be a standard technique to keep her off the defensive.

"Well, I'm getting a little tired of waiting for things to happen here. I want to know what's going on."

"You're not getting cold feet, are you?"

Damnation. Is that all you care about? It's not whether I'm sane or not or even if I'll stay sane through the trial. Just as long as I don't back out. As long as I don't let them down. I guess that's her role, to be sure the witnesses are at the trial. Well, dammit, if I appear or not it is by my choice, and you had better get me the answers I need instead of all your empty reassurances. You've never testified. You've never been raped. So just get me in touch with the lawyer who has some answers and stop wasting my time.

I was switched over to a Mr. Upchurch who was handling the case. He had a gentle voice and seemed interested in talking to me.

"I can understand why you're impatient, Mrs. Barr. Can we get together tomorrow afternoon about it?"

"Sure." I felt calm and confident that I had finally gotten past Ms. Parrish. Now there was someone to really listen to me, someone with some answers. He had a stake in the case, too. He would have to listen.

During the two-hour talk with Mr. Upchurch, most of my questions came down to, "What evidence is there?" "Why should anyone believe me?"

"Now, Mrs. Barr, it doesn't matter what other evidence

there is besides your testimony. Your testimony is enough."

It didn't jive with all I'd ever heard about rape trials. There was no medical report, no witnesses. Mr. Upchurch even said he didn't think he'd use the slides of the cuts on my side. "They weren't very dramatic." But they showed he had a knife, that he wasn't afraid to use it, they showed that it was by force. Isn't that a basic ingredient that had to be proven for rape? "Why would anyone believe it even happened?"

"Mrs. Barr. This is a very obvious case. I've handled some really sticky ones, and this is the most straightforward case of rape that I've seen. I can't even imagine what his defense will be. I'm surprised he hasn't pleaded guilty. He still can, of course. The only defense I can imagine is mistaken identity, but I can't see what could be done with that. It is obvious that he is the guy. You're sure. The police were sure. I don't know why this case is going to court, but I assure you, Mrs. Barr, it is a very straightforward case. You just tell your story and say that's the guy who did it. We don't need anything more."

"But why would they believe me?" I pressed.

"Why not? It's a simple case. You had no contact with him before. No 'provocative behavior.' You weren't intoxicated or using drugs. You reported it immediately to the police. You're happily married."

"What about the gap in information to the police? My going back later with additional information that changed the charge to rape?"

"No problem. You didn't change your story, you just added to it. It fit in with the original information. The police slipped in the interview. They should never haved allowed your statement of 'he masturbated' to just go by. Obviously he had to masturbate against something, his hand, your hand, your body. The police should have asked you during the first interview."

Don't blame Jameson. He was so good to me. Nobody could have pushed me for information that day. It wasn't Jameson, it was me. A person can only do so much and he got more information out of me by his gentleness than anyone else could have.

Mr. Upchurch spent a lot of time talking about other cases he had had, interesting but irrelevant. Between his stories I got enough pieces of information to satisfy me for the moment.

The other cases would not be pursued; the women had been on the subpoena just to leave that option open. Mr. Upchurch had already talked to them about it. It was just an oversight that Officer Burke was not on the subpoena. He would testify. Mr. Upchurch explained the ingredients of the laws to me:

Rape was "sexual intercourse against the will and consent of the other person by force or threat of force." It was obviously against my will, but could I *prove* it was against my will? It was obviously by force, click on the slides on my cuts, but they weren't dramatic enough to use. But the key ingredient, sexual intercourse, could I swear it was intercourse? No, I couldn't say it was. I never said it was. The police, the state, said it was. I could only say what happened and let them decide. Maximum sentence: life.

Assault with Intent to Rape was the second charge. Obviously assault, if they believed any of my story. How could anyone prove intent to anything unless it was carried out?

"Well, it's a charge that always goes along with rape. And he obviously intended to rape you, that's why he grabbed you. He didn't rob you or show any intent or thought of robbery. If rape crossed his mind for even a moment, it is intent to rape and it obviously crossed his mind." Obviously? Who can say what would cross a mind like that? Why not add intent to murder, I felt that as much as rape. Maximum sentence: thirty years.

In the Perverted Sex Acts charge, force or consent were not ingredients, just unnatural sexual acts, anything besides intercourse. Obviously it fit that category, but again, I had no proof. Maximum sentence: ten years—"a sentence rarely given. It's an archaic law."

Assault and Battery were two separate charges. Assault was the threat of force, battery was carrying it out. I wasn't battered. "But you had bruises; if he laid a hand on you, it's battery and he did more than that." Yeah, that's true. I thought assault and battery was being beaten up, but I had to accept his interpretations. Maximum sentence: indefinite. "One case a few years ago got twenty years in a very serious case. It's up to the judge."

Translation of it all: If he was found guilty of the most unnatural and perverted sexual acts, even with the threat of violence and against the consent of the victim, he could get ten years. But if they said it was rape, he could get life plus thirty years. Even if he just tried to rape me but didn't, he could get three times the sentence he'd get for carrying out his perverted sex acts. Somehow that seemed a bit absurd. Rape was a major crime, but the most atrocious perverted sex acts were a minor offense. It would have been much simpler at the time and for the trial, if it had been simple classic rape. How could the law make such a huge differentiation between "sexual assault" and "rape"? I just hoped that that little slip of his penis did constitute rape, that the police and the state were right. It wasn't the difference in the sentence that meant so much. I just couldn't tolerate the implication of "You weren't raped; it was only a minor mishap."

But Upchurch was confident there would be no problem with any of the charges.

JOURNAL - October 8, Friday

What a cruddy day. It's raining. I feel very unorganized. Jon went to work huffy because I said the lawn needs mowing. I shouldn't make comments like that on rainy days. I'm tired of housecleaning, over and over. If I could get organized and not have this constant mess. I want to do things right and all I do is the dishes. Jon was mad that I got home so late from seeing Upchurch, then grumbled that I went grocery shopping. "You should do that during the day." He wanted a quiet evening at home with me. How should I know that unless he tells me?

Upchurch was nice but I'm not sure he understands. Maybe he doesn't have to understand as long as he's a good lawyer. But it's not just winning or losing the case. I want to survive this thing. I have to feel confident, not just in the case but in me. I'm not just a piece of evidence. It would be fine if I just had to hand in a written report. The cold facts. ". . . your poetic report." That's what he called my write-up for the police where I thought I did a good job of just the facts, ma'am. "You sound like a frustrated poet." (1) Oh, no, not at all, Mr. Upchurch. There isn't a rhyme in it. Nor reason, only facts. Simply stated. Simplicity does make good poetry. (2) I'm not frustrated at all. The report was only one of my nicer works. You should read some of my application forms for real poetry. (3) I'm not frustrated. Writing things I can't say relieves frustration. A strike against you if you don't appreciate lucid descriptions. Do you realize how hard I worked to eliminate my emotions and stick to facts! "Poetic report"! I forget that I was only a witness, a happenstance of the case, a piece of evidence. Garbage cans don't emote, they just display their dents. I forget so easily.

There were practical plans I needed to make for the week of the trial. Someone to take care of the kids. I wanted Rosemary with me, so my normal sitter wouldn't do. Mom had just gone back to work, but maybe something could be arranged with her or Michelle. The kids were comfortable with them, and it would be good if the kids could stay there away from the tension. I called and talked to both Michelle and Mom.

"Hi, Michelle. What are you doing with the kids now that Mom is working? . . . Oh, that's a shame that you've had to take off work, but you think this sitter will work out? . . . Oh, I see. Well, I'm glad to hear things are working out. Uh, is Mom there?

"How's your job going, Mom? . . . Sounds like you have pretty flexible hours if you're planning to take time off when Dana's baby arrives. . . . Yeah, it would be good if it comes on a weekend and you could take a couple long weekends. . . . Do you think you could come spend the weekend with us the weekend before the twenty-seventh? . . . Sure, I understand that you'd like to help them get ready for the baby. It's not due till Thanksgiving,

is it? . . . Yeah, of course, if you've made plans with them
for that weekend. . . . How am I doing? I, uh . . . oh no,
we don't have any colds or anything." I thought for a moment she cared, for a moment I thought she might even be
aware of what was going on in my life. If I was getting married or expecting a baby in two weeks, she would certainly
be over here or calling every other day! How foolish of me
to think she might be any help baby-sitting. Even thinking
she might help me clean the house and feel organized for
the trial. Why should I expect her to remember something
so trite as a trial when my brother's wife was going to have a
baby. After all, she couldn't possibly wait another weekend
before going up to help them prepare the nursery for a baby
due in six weeks. Of course, after promising them she'd be
there that weekend, they'd never forgive her if she changed
her plans to come and help me. Such a reliable help when I
needed her! I wasn't even asking for impossible moral support, just help in cleaning. She was certainly capable of that.
I was furiously let down. Maybe I was too sensitive, maybe
other people could have accepted it, but I felt turned out in
the cold. I wanted to scream at her on the phone, but I
knew my words had to be carefully planned because I probably wouldn't be able to get many out. Something had to be
said to her though, I wouldn't let this pass. After the trial,
after dealing with that ordeal, I'd work on the rest.

A math test that night kept my mind off more important things. I could solve those problems, I could get answers, I could get acknowledgment that I knew what I was
talking about. I was glad it was a test night. Quiet concentration in an impartial classroom was what my mind needed.
I could stare into space with an acceptable reason. The

math came too mechanically to distract my thoughts. I watched the instructor stoop to check the time by the clock in the hall. It was nice he had a clock this semester. He could never keep track of time last term because he lost watches. Time was running out. I had to watch the clock too. The clock on the wall was so obvious, hanging above the door where the judge could see it easily. Would I want to know what time it was? How long it would take? It was seven-forty-six by the clock in the green delivery room even though the birth certificate says seven-forty-five. Time is important. I was the first one to hand in my test, and I paced the empty halls waiting for class to resume.

JOURNAL - October 15, Friday

A year ago today—only a year? It seems like a lifetime. Already a year? The memories are still so vivid. It seems like I can remember every leaf on the trees even. The weather wasn't too different than today. The autumn colors were prettier than this year. A year ago I thought it was all over with. It would never have occurred to me that a year later I would be getting ready for a trial. I was waiting for the morning to have it all behind me and forgotten.

JOURNAL - October 16, Saturday

It is beginning to hit me. Small problems and pressures seem unmanageable. I want someone to take over. I have to find a baby-sitter for Monday's class. Go away all of you dumb problems. Who's going to baby-sit during the trial? What am I going to wear? When can I go shopping? I must have new shoes. I need an outfit I feel good in. I need a

clean house. Everyone leave me alone, don't expect anything
from me. No, don't leave me alone, take over for me. I can't
fix lunch, we have no bread.

On Monday of the week before the trial, I called Mr.
Upchurch and asked if we could get together again. "I
thought we covered everything last time."

"Well, I don't feel comfortable about it. I need more
answers."

"I don't think I can tell you any more than I have."

I felt shaky and uncertain of my voice. I wasn't sure
what I needed but things seemed too vague. I couldn't think
of any important questions, but I wasn't sure he had my
whole story. He had the "poetic report" I'd written for the
police, but I had gone over more details with Ms. Parrish.
She didn't take any notes; had those details gotten to Mr.
Upchurch? I felt uncertain of what was happening. I
thought Mr. Upchurch was planning to talk to me again before the trial. I didn't know our one talk three weeks before
the trial would be our sole contact. I had to depend on him,
I had to trust him, but I hardly knew him and I didn't know
how much he knew. I didn't know what his case would be. I
didn't know what my case would be. He didn't want to talk
to me any more before the trial.

"But I . . . I mean . . . I don't know the case. . . .
What do I say? I've never been in a trial. . . . I mean, I just
don't know what's going on."

"Listen, Mrs. Barr, we went over everything when you
were in here. Two hours is more than I spend with most
witnesses. All you have to do is answer questions."

JOURNAL - October 20, Wednesday

I'm getting paranoid again. I feel like I'm being manipulated by the State's attorney's office. It's all out of my control,
just do what they tell me. Don't get out of line 'cause there
is a knife in my ribs. I've been through all this before. I'm
being used again to satisfy someone's ego. *They* are going to
win this case because *they* have such a good witness. Here I
am, the ideal victim—articulate, sane, moral, no devious behavior. What the hell is their case anyway? Why the
hell don't they just say "We could lose the case"? Why
should the jury believe me? The truth can't be judged on my
poise, on my wits, on my dress. The truth *can* be helped by
evidence. Where is such evidence? If I was paying Upchurch to represent me, he'd listen to me. I don't even have
a choice of attorney. Mr. Rapist can hire the best lawyer in
the country and you can be sure his lawyer is working on
the case. What kind of justice is this? I have no rights in this
at all, not even the right to be listened to. My two-page report isn't the whole story, you know. The defense usually
asks questions. Don't you want to discuss that part? Don't
you want to know the details? "It's such a straightforward
case." You expect to just walk into court on October 27 to
find out it might not be so straightforward? This case could
be lost, Mr. Upchurch! It might not matter to you but it
matters to me and it matters to his next victims if they survive. It matters, Mr. Upchurch!

Jon was concerned about my frustrations and called
Mr. Upchurch himself. He said Upchurch was on the defensive, saying that he knows best how to proceed. Don't ask
questions. He suggested that if I had more questions I

should talk to Ms. Parrish and she could record the conversation for him.

I called Ms. Parrish and did not keep my normal cool. "I want someone to listen to me!"

"Mrs. Barr, calm down now. We can handle this. . . . You're getting yourself all worked up over nothing. . . ."

"Ms. Parrish, if Upchurch won't listen to me, he won't have any trial to worry about." I had pulled the trump I'd forgotten I had.

"Well, if you really feel like you need it, I'll talk to Mr. Upchurch and see if we can set up an appointment to talk to him. I'll arrange to be there too if it would help."

She heard me this time. The reassuring tone had changed to concern. Perhaps it wasn't concern for me, perhaps it was concern for the case, for justice or for her job, but there was a concern that I hadn't heard from her before.

I called Karen to go with me. I wasn't sure I was up to delivering my trump alone. She knew the questions I needed answers to.

JOURNAL - October 21, Thursday

I want to know what the case is. I KNOW what the truth is! God, reading over my "poetic report," some poetry! It couldn't have happened. How can I possibly say it in court? I can't even read it without cringing, shaking, my stomach in my throat. What the hell am I going through this for?!

He put me through hell once. What wonderful justice for me to go through hell again, so he can get a slap on the wrist. Hell, even if he gets ten years, he'll be out on parole in three or less. That is not punishment for what I've been through. If the case is lost or a light sentence is given, then

I've been through hell for a good show for the judge and jury and they'll all go home to their lovely homes while I rot. There is no justice. Why pretend? Why go through with this farce? I hope there is an ultimate justice. Somehow it *has* to make a difference.

I was caught between destructive forces. To bring myself out of my depression, I had been trying to build my self-confidence. If I had no self-confidence, I would crumble under cross-examination. If I had no feeling that I was a worthwhile being, I would be putty in the hands of the defense. So I had come out of my depression, convincing myself that I was a human entitled to respect. Now I had to deal with the State telling me I was just a body. Just appear. They didn't care who I was, or what I thought or believed in, just submit your evidence. I couldn't accept such a totally passive role. I wanted to do everything I possibly could to help the case. I didn't want to have any regrets after the case was lost that I could have done something more. I had to try in spite of the opposition. I felt exhausted and defeated by the State, but I had gotten an appointment to get into the office and maybe this time someone would listen.

Karen and I arrived at the courthouse early on Friday, so we sat in the hall with cups of coffee. Having asserted myself to get there, I wasn't sure why or what I would say. We talked about the questions that needed answers and my reason for being there seemed clearer. A wedding party joyfully passed us as we waited. We looked at each other in astonishment. "In the same building even. Unreal."

Ms. Parrish met us and ushered us to a private office.

"Mr. Upchurch had an appointment this morning, so he suggested we tape our conversation."

I hadn't won after all.

"He gave me a copy of all the questions he plans to ask you. So we can go over those."

Perhaps not a total loss.

Ms. Parrish was more subdued than normal. Perhaps facing two of us, she was somewhat intimidated. Perhaps feeling caught in between, she was out of her element. She wasn't at her desk, quoting her lines. She was playing the lawyer. She wasn't full of her reassurances; she had a more important role to pursue.

"Let's take this as though you were testifying now. I'll go through Mr. Upchurch's questions. Take your time in telling the story."

I had been prepared to talk about testifying. On this trip to the courthouse, I wasn't prepared to tell the whole story. The assault seemed so distant. I had been thinking so much about the trial I hadn't been remembering the details.

"O.K. Let's go over the story."

I took a deep breath, licked my lips and began. I didn't feel that I could remember anything. I was trying too hard; it all seemed unreal, like describing a movie second by second.

"You're doing fine, Jennifer." I had forgotten Karen was there until she patted my arm.

I was exhausted and confused when I finished and was ready to leave, but Karen pursued my concerns.

"There has really been a communications gap with Jennifer. It seems that your office might be able to handle things more smoothly. She has gotten conflicting information from different sources and hasn't gotten many straight answers."

I heard what Karen was saying as I tried to get my strength back. I was glad she was trying to speak up for me, but she wasn't saying it right. That wasn't really the issue. I appreciated her effort, and if she hadn't spoken up, I would never have found the energy or courage to say what I was really feeling.

"No. It's more than that." I spoke with clenched fists and not looking up. "I am feeling totally powerless, totally manipulated. I've been through this before—at knife point. I don't need to be raped by the courts. . . . I don't need to be treated . . ." My tears were in full flow, but I continued talking in a rigidly controlled voice, my anger and frustration beginning to overflow. ". . . I do not need to be kicked around anymore. Someone has got to treat me like a human sometime. I am not an object. I am not a set of finger prints to be filed away till you need me. . . . I am not a piece of trash! I just want to be treated like a person! That's all. I do not need to be raped again by the system." I stopped and looked at Karen. She had tears in her eyes. I was afraid to look at Ms. Parrish. "You can't understand. You don't know what it's like to be a cigarette butt. I'm sorry I just can't stand it anymore!" It was foolish to have tried to explain. I was angry that I wasted my energy.

"It's O.K., Jennifer." Even Karen didn't come forth with her reassurances, just "It's O.K."

No one talked for an endless length of time. What could they say? How can anyone argue with irrational statements? But my body felt better that I'd finally vomited.

Ms. Parrish turned to Karen. "Well . . . Can I do anything more for you?"

Karen brought up the questions about evidence, about what the case would consist of. I listened. There was some evidence—there was a case besides my testimony. They had found the clothes I'd described, and more important they had found the unusual knife. To refresh my memory, I looked at the copy of my composite picture that was in the file. We left with a feeling that the effort had been worth it.

"That was beautiful, Jennifer," Karen said as we walked out to the car.

"My story? Yeah, lovely."

"No, Jennifer." She knew I wasn't serious. "What you said. My God, you said it."

"What did I say?"

"You said what every rape victim feels but can't put into words. And she heard it; she was at a loss for words. Ms. Parrish is *never* at a loss for words, I can assure you. It really hit her hard, and I don't think she'll forget it easily. Not the way you said it."

Do you really think so, Karen? Did I really get the message across to somebody? If she got the message, if she understood—no, that was too much to ask. But maybe she'd recognize it if she saw it in another victim. Maybe—well, I tried.

That night memories of the incident became more vivid. The straining I had done that day to remember the details had pulled it painfully back. Every detail was there as if it had just happened. The memories were sharp and just as important, the gaps in my memory were defined. I wouldn't be confused by trying to guess an answer for something I didn't remember. As the details went through my head, I suddenly realized that the composite picture Mr. Upchurch had was not the one I had done. I had drawn in some details myself that weren't on that drawing. That was the picture the previous victim had done. I'd have to call Detective Jameson to have him check on that.

I was up quite late, but with the help of Valium throughout the weekend, I did get some sleep.

CHAPTER XI

"HELLO, Mrs. Barr? This is Hillary Parrish. We just learned that the defendant has decided on a trial by judge instead of by jury, so the jury was dismissed today. I thought you'd like to know. I hope it makes it easier for you."

Thank you. Thank you for telling me. For remembering me. For thinking it might matter to me. Was it a sign that he was scared, that he might plead guilty? I was ready to testify now. I had put a lot of energy in preparing for it. It would have been a letdown if he pleaded guilty. But no jury. The jury has been dismissed. For sure, no jury. The whole scene changed. So much fear and worry about the jury. I hadn't even thought about facing a judge. It seemed so much easier. It almost seemed too simple. With no jury to select and to deliberate, the trial might even be over in one day. It could be all over; I might even know the outcome by the next evening.

A lot of people called that day. It helped the day pass and was reassuring. Margot called to ask if I would mind if she came to the trial.

"Listen, Jennifer. I know you'll do a great job, and don't worry. I really feel like they have such a case on this guy that they won't have any problem with any of the charges. I probably shouldn't say that, but I feel so sure. I can't see how he could possibly get off."

Margot thinks that too, huh. She knew the story better than anyone else. She knew all my doubts, all the things I couldn't verbalize to others. I wasn't feeling that sure of the outcome, but I didn't want to think about it. I could only think of getting through my testimony. A month ago I had thought about how I would feel if he got off, but I couldn't think of it now. How could anyone feel sure what would happen?

That night Jon helped me clean the house. It was important to have it spotless, to have something under control. The kids were rambunctious, but I tried to deal with them calmly. I didn't want them more upset than necessary.

"Nigel, it is very important for you to go to bed quietly tonight. Papa and I are very nervous because of the trial tomorrow."

"Why are you talking like Aunt Michelle, Mama?"

"Like Aunt Michelle? How am I like Aunt Michelle?"

"I can't hear you talking. Talk loud like *you* do."

Was that a commentary on my mothering or just on the past weeks, months, year—most of his memory?

"Are you scared, Mama? Will the bad man be there?"

"Yes, I am nervous about tomorrow, but the bad man won't hurt me." I wanted to explain more, but I didn't think he could understand about truth, justice, and judgments.

"He broke the law, like when you break a rule, but because he is a grown man it is more serious. That's why they have a trial to hear all the eviden—to see whether he really did it or not. If they decide that he was very bad, they will punish him. But tomorrow they must decide. That's why I have to go to tell what happened to me." I wasn't sure I had explained anything.

"Did you have your shoes on?"

"Shoes?"

"When you walked in the woods?"

I couldn't imagine how he knew that detail. He had overheard more than I ever remembered saying.

"Will he get worse than a spanking? Will he get killed?"

"No, he'll probably have to go to jail."

"Once when I went for a walk with just my shoes on and I told Colin he couldn't come but I was sorry I didn't let him because a big huge dog with a hat on, you know, grabbed me and ate me up but the police put him in a tiny little cage without any doors, you know, and put it inside a big box and threw it away but I got out and came home 'cause I was brave."

Perhaps I'd been trying to communicate with the wrong people. I had been trying to communicate with words to people who only understood words. Sometimes the words aren't what needs to be communicated.

Later I heard Nigel trying to quiet Colin by explaining why they had to be quiet. He told some more variations of

his dog story and I heard Colin's "Oh," in each pause between stories. Finally they were quiet and I peeked in. Nigel
was asleep, cuddling his Snoopy, and Colin was lying on his
back, staring wide-eyed at the ceiling. I didn't dare try to
imagine what was going through my toddler's head.

JOURNAL - October 26, Tuesday
The incident seems so vague, so far away tonight. I'm so
nervous and should review my notes. It's tomorrow—the
final step. It will be over. After so long, so many lives, so
many torments. The final torment. Everything seems too
calm and organized. Isn't there something I should be worrying about, something I can worry about? What a dumb
soap opera. This isn't really happening. Is this me? No, it
can't be. I can't believe tomorrow will happen. Can't I find
something to cry about? I wish this would be over with. It
can't really be happening.

Mr. Upchurch had asked me to be at the courthouse at
nine-thirty even though the trial was scheduled for ten. Jon,
Rosemary, and I were ready to leave by eight-forty-five and
waited in suspended animation for the baby-sitter to arrive
at nine.

When we arrived at the courthouse, the halls were
crowded and I recognized some friends from the Crisis Center. I was glad to see them, but I just nodded as I passed.
Detective Jameson was in Mr. Upchurch's office and they
stood when we came in. Jameson sat on a table in the corner
of the office.

"Did you find my composite picture?"

"No, but it doesn't matter that much. It's not supposed

to be a photograph; it is just a guideline for the police." He spoke slowly and looked at me gently.

Karen came into the office soon after we did. She gave me a hug and I assured her I was O.K. I smoked a lot and paced a lot, anxious to get underway. Mr. Upchurch went into the courtroom to see what was happening. When he returned, he said everything was ready and we should go in.

As we passed through the doors, the room was still. The judge was at his bench and the pews were filled with people. I knew where the defendant's table was and avoided looking that way. I realized abruptly that I was going directly to the stand.

"Please stand and raise your right hand."

My mind wasn't there yet. I followed directions.

"Please be seated and state your name and address."

My address? I hesitated.

"It's for the record, ma'am."

I complied. Mr. Upchurch stood and began questions.

"How long have you lived in this county? Who do you live with? . . . Can you state the ages of your children? . . ."

What does that have to do with anything? But I answered. Mr. Upchurch was on my side.

"Were you at your home on Thursday, October 15, 1975?"

"It was Wednesday, October 15."

"Yes, well, were you home on that day?"

"In the morning, I was home. I mean, before I went out."

"Did you have occasion to leave your home on that day?"

"Yes." I said I did. Didn't I just say I did?

"Why? Where did you go? Why did you go there? . . . How did you get there? . . . What did you do then? . . . Did you see anyone else there? . . ."

I struggled to follow his questions and give correct answers. I wasn't thinking of that day, I was reciting what I'd gone over enough times that the answers were obvious. I was trying to grasp where I was. What was I doing there? *Wait, everybody wait, till I find out where I am.* My head was spinning, the room was a yellow haze, there were no sounds except the questions and my voice. I twisted my ring, shifted my feet, and when I glanced up, it was to the empty jury box. I had no idea who else was present in the room.

"Do you see that person in the courtroom? . . . The person who grabbed you, do you see him here today?"

I slowly raised my head and turned toward the defendant's table. I saw Jon and Rosemary sitting directly behind Mr. Upchurch. My eyes came to rest on the defendant. I had seen him twice before. He was the man I had seen in the lineup. My eyes froze, the room dissolved. It was that man and me, alone again. The woods, the hatred enveloped us, and terror was pounding in my head.

"Mrs. Barr, the microphone cannot pick up a nod. You must answer yes or no." I think the words came from the judge. The defendant stared back at me and smirked. My jaw set, my chest heaved. "Yes. . . . Yes, your honor." I felt as if the words were shouted.

"Can you describe the man you have pointed out? Did you understand the question, Mrs. Barr? Can you tell us where you indicated he is sitting? What he is wearing?"

"Brown suit. He's at the table with a brown suit. He's sitting over there." *God, why are you making me do this? You know who I'm talking about! You know who the accused is? Who else would I be talking about? You want me to go down and hold him up for you? God, what do you want!*

"Let the record show that she pointed out the defendant. . . ."

"Objection, your honor." Mr. Canfield rose behind the defendant's table. "This witness has said nothing to show that she even saw the man who grabbed her except for a passing glance. Is she identifying him from that? I maintain she is identifying him from the lineup."

There was a long discussion. It seemed to me that the defense lawyer was right. I should have given a description of the man who grabbed me before pointing him out in court. After all when it came time to state my description, I could just look down at that guy and say anything that fit. The lawyers' arguments didn't seem to have anything to do with that point, and I didn't try to follow it. I was trying to erase his smirk from my mind.

"Now, Mrs. Barr. After the accused grabbed you . . ."

"Objection . . ." The defense.

"Sustained." The judge.

"O.K. After you were grabbed, did the man who grabbed you say anything?"

"Objection. Leading the witness."

"After you were grabbed, what happened?"

I couldn't remember which question had been left intact.

"Mrs. Barr, can you answer the question?" The judge.

"He said . . . I screamed . . . so he said 'shut up' . . ."

"Did he say anything more?"

"Objection."

"Sustained. Rephrase your question."

"O.K. Was there anything unusual about his voice? Anything you noticed at this time?"

Will you all leave me alone! I hadn't finished saying what I was saying, and now you say I can't say it because he asked me to say it? Does anyone here even want to hear what happened?

The questions continued and it was established that a knife was held at my throat.

"Could you identify that knife?"

"Yes."

"Objection. She hasn't even established that she saw it."

"Sustained."

What does sustained mean anyway? I waited for Mr. Upchurch to ask again. If he didn't, I guessed the question stood as it was, whatever it was.

"Mrs. Barr, did you see a knife?"

"Yes."

"Can you describe what you saw."

"He pulled something out of his pocket, and when he opened it, I saw it was a knife."

"How long was it?"

"I couldn't tell. . . . I wasn't thinking of that. . . . It was a knife."

"How did you describe the knife to the police?"

"I showed them with my hands, like this long. . . ."

"About four to five inches?"

"Yes, I guess that's about what I said."

"That was the blade you were talking about?"

"Objection."

"Overruled."

"I only saw the blade at that point. I didn't see any of the rest of it till later." I had forgotten the question, but it was something about the description of the knife.

"Is this the knife you saw?" He held up an object.

"Objection, she couldn't know if that was *the* knife she saw."

"Sustained."

"Does this look like the knife you saw?"

"Objection . . ."

"I'll rephrase. Have you ever seen an object that looked like this before?"

"That looks like the knife that was held at my throat but I . . ."

"Objection, any knife would look like a knife. How could she identify it by the blade?"

Can I tell you about the knife? Can I say what I observed later when I had a chance to examine it? I certainly couldn't identify it from those first moments of panic. I can't swear that was the knife that was held at my throat. If I could see it better, if Upchurch would stop gripping the handle and let me see the whole thing, I could say if it was the knife I saw later on the ground. But we were not there yet.

Upchurch heard at least some of my thoughts. He came and stood in front of me, fidgeting with the knife as the technical discussion continued. Finally the knife was admitted for identification purposes. The knife did not become an issue again; the defense didn't allow it to enter the testimony. "Knife" was the magic word that brought the defense lawyer to his feet and "objection" to his lips. I wasn't sure what had even been communicated about it.

The story was picked up again. My lips cracked when I spoke. I felt so confused and my body strained to understand each question. Mr. Upchurch's questions were not in the correct order, and in my answers I kept trying to keep the story straight. I tried to push to get my mind back to that time and that place, to recall the scene accurately, but when I was forced to jump ahead or back, the rerun got scrambled. I felt as if my mind was going to quit under the strain. It was sputtering in confusion when I became aware of someone entering the courtroom. I glanced back and saw Ava in a bright orange dress. Suddenly my head was still. Truth. That's all I'm here for. To tell what happened. I have nothing to fear. There is a greater justice than this. The truth will come through this confusion and distortion. They are playing word games, but I don't have to play. The questions began to make more sense. I allowed my mind to turn off whenever the defense counsel stood. I didn't try to understand what they were doing. I didn't even try to listen.

Describing the sexual details was very difficult. I was afraid the ring I was twisting on my finger would melt from the pressure and heat. A court clerk offered me water and Kleenex. She seemed very concerned about me, and I fell in love with her at first notice.

Step by step, every move was questioned. "Where was his hand at that point?" "How far were you from the lake?" "Were you kneeling or lying down at that point?" "Was he behind you or beside you?" "Did he say that before or after he stood up?" Finally the story ended. I wasn't sure what had been said, but it was over.

Mr. Upchurch pulled out some clothing for me to identify. They had the right shoes, but the pants were not the same.

The judge called a ten-minute recess before the defense began its cross-examination.

I turned to the helpful clerk as soon as the judge stepped down. "Where can I have a cigarette?"

"You can go out to the hall, but don't talk to anyone about the case."

As I walked out, Jon and Rosemary joined me. Jon gave me a hug but said nothing. The hall was small and crowded. I found an ashtray and squatted down beside it. I couldn't trust my legs to stand, there were no chairs and I wanted to be below eye level. I leaned my head against the wall and stared straight ahead. I saw Jameson and Burke standing at the end of the hall. They were both watching me and nodded. I heard Margot say, "You're doing fine, Jennifer. Just great." Someone patted my head. I was in my own world, only partly aware of who was with me. My mind took a total break from all thoughts.

I was afraid of the cross-examination because I didn't know what to expect, but I was feeling a sense of relief that I had gotten through the story and would not have to detail it again. When I took the stand again, the defense attorney seemed sensitive to what had happened to me and didn't try to challenge the event. When it was obvious that it was the identification he was challenging, my confidence rose. I had taken great care with the identification. I was sure.

He pursued my memory of details, the identification to the police, the lineup.

"Now, Mrs. Barr, isn't it possible that just because this man has the same features as the man who attacked you, that this is not the right man?"

What an absurd question! Mr. Upchurch stood up. A legal discussion ended in an overruled objection, but Canfield had forgotten his question. "This was a very important question, Your Honor, and she was about to give me the answer I wanted to hear. Can the record be read back so I can remember the question?"

I remembered the question perfectly but I didn't want to aid the enemy. *What answer was it that I was about to give that was the answer he wanted? I must have nodded my head, but my nodding was for the confirmation of my opinion of the defense. Of course, it was possible, anything is possible. There is a one in ten million possibility, but yes, certainly a possibility.*

The question was read back and I was ready to answer.

"If it is possible for two people to have exactly the same features, it is possible it is not the same man." I felt it was a strong, definite statement, stated in a confident voice. He looked shocked and quickly retreated to other details.

"You saw Detective Jameson right after the incident. Can you tell me what he was wearing on that day?"

"I saw him a day after the incident. . . ." But Upchurch objected that it was irrelevant.

"She seems very capable of determining what is relevant and what is irrelevant herself, but it is good of you to help her out, Mr. Upchurch. Objection sustained." I wasn't sure how to interpret the judge's commentary. Was he put-

ting me down or Upchurch or neither or both? I had been
warned before the trial to answer the questions directly, or
the judge might reprimand me. He hadn't, but I had been
careful to stick to the questions until they started getting absurd. I wanted to answer the question. It would have allowed me to elaborate, "I didn't make a point of studying
Jameson *the way I studied my assailant.*" I was beginning to
catch on to the game. I had been the State's pawn but I
wouldn't let the defense manipulate me.

"Mrs. Barr, isn't it true that you felt you were expected
to pick someone out of the lineup and this man was the
closest resemblance? Just answer yes or no."

I boldly took advantage of the door he opened for a
lengthy description of the doubts and the feelings of responsibility that had weighed on me on the weekend before the
lineup. I had gone over very carefully all that I positively
remembered and all the implications of an identification. I
did not fit a yes or a no in my answer. The judge did not
reprimand me.

The attorney's sympathetic attitude had definitely disappeared. I didn't have to stretch my imagination to feel
that he was beginning to detest me.

Again he went back to the features I had based my
identification on. "You only saw your assailant with a hat
and sunglasses on. How could you possibly base an
identification on a nose?"

My patience with that subject evaporated. We had
gone over and over how I had identified him, what definite
features I had reported to the police, the features I had
studied and memorized, the features I had observed at the
lineup. I was positive, and I had explained why and how I

was positive. Did he expect me to suddenly say, You're right, I couldn't possibly identify him? I wouldn't have gone through that morning if I wasn't positive. I had been on the stand for two hours and he expected to start at the beginning again?

"I am positive! I did not see his eyes, that is true." I spoke slowly with emphasis on each word. "I had studied his mouth, his jaw, his nose, his cheeks, his chin, his ears, his skin. Every feature I observed in the man on October 15, last year, I saw in this man on June 1, this year, at the lineup." My voice rose in frustration of how to get the point across. "If he had had a bag over his head down to his eyes, I could have identified him! There is more to a face than just eyes! I know it is the same man!"

The subject was finally closed and soon after that the cross-examination was finished.

"Before you step down, Mrs. Barr, I'd like to have one point clarified for me." The judge spoke and I turned to him. He had seemed so far away on his high bench, but when I turned to speak directly to him, he leaned over and I felt suddenly as if I wasn't being judged, that he wasn't a judge, he was someone who wanted to talk to me. "I know it has been a long, exhausting morning for you, but I need some details explained. Can you tell me precisely if his penis entered your vagina at any point?"

This was the question the rape charge hinged on. It had not been addressed by either lawyer. The defense hadn't argued the point, but the judge wanted it to be clear so that he could decide whether or not it was rape. I was glad he was concerned; the question would be carefully considered and my mind could be settled on the matter.

I explained as well as I could, but we weren't using the same language. I didn't understand his terms and he didn't understand mine. I was getting very frustrated. "If I had a diagram I could show you, but I don't know how to explain any better."

"I know it's very difficult for you, but since you have two children, it is obvious you have had intercourse. Can you explain how that is the same or different from what happened?"

I intensely wanted him to understand, but I couldn't find more explicit words. He wanted to understand too, but we were frustrated by a stand-off. He seemed very sympathetic and understanding of my situation. Though I was sitting there discussing sex with a judge in front of a roomful of people, I was not intimidated, I wasn't even embarrassed. I was oblivious of my audience and the judge was a person struggling with me.

I was finally dismissed from the stand and a lunch break was called. As I left the courtroom, I was surrounded by people touching me and saying what a great job I'd done. I was numb but smiled instinctively. Jon, Rosemary, and Ava followed me down to the coffee machines and waited on me as I slowly returned to an awareness of my surroundings that I had had to repress in the courtroom. I reviewed my more triumphant moments and glowed in the knowledge that I had made it through my testimony. I felt good about the cross-examination testimony. It was over.

I wanted to go outside and everyone else wanted lunch, so we walked downtown. The fresh air seemed a special gift, though I felt weak and slightly nauseous.

The trial resumed at two o'clock, so we met Mr. Upchurch slightly before then. I was told to wait in the State's attorney's office for the rest of the day, but there were no quiet corners there. When I refused to wait there, he agreed to allow me to wait out the day in a large grand jury room on the top floor. I found quiet and privacy there, quiet and privacy like a museum at midnight. Rosemary stayed with me when Jon and Ava went down to the trial. I wanted Jon to be able to report back to me when the trial was over. I had taken my math and some knitting to fill the time, but I never touched either. Since we were not allowed to talk about the trial, we picked up trivial topics to toss back and forth till we both laughed about their triviality and then there was silence.

After about an hour of waiting, Jon came up and said I was needed back on the stand. I was stunned. I wasn't prepared to go back. I had finished what I had to do. What now? What more did they want to ask me?

"Mrs. Barr, you are still under oath. Please be seated." *Of course, do you expect me to change my story at this point?*

"Mrs. Barr, did you speak to Detective Jameson again after your interview on October 16?"

"Objection."

Mr. Upchurch rephrased the question a few more times.

I was confused, but all he seemed to want to know was whether I had talked to Detective Jameson in January and about what.

"Yes I saw Detective Jameson in January to fill in details that I couldn't say the first time we met."

"And what details were those?"

I took a deep breath. "I had described certain acts as masturbating during the first interview. I filled in the details that I went over with the judge this morning—that part of his masturbating was rubbing against me—my—like I said this morning."

"Thank you, Mrs. Barr. The prosecution rests."

"Now, Mrs. Barr, three months after the fact, you have the police change the charge to rape." The defense seemed to be fired with a new confidence. "Why didn't you tell Detective Jameson this during the first interview if that was actually what happened?"

"It was very difficult for me to talk about it at all." *Do I say I didn't think it was rape? I didn't ask for the charge to be changed to rape? I didn't know the definition of rape? I didn't think it was important?* My mind wasn't thinking fast enough to consider the implications of any of those answers, so I didn't try to explain further. I wished Upchurch had discussed this point with me earlier. He said there was no problem, but I didn't know how to respond, what interpretation could be put on what I said.

"What made you change your mind during this time?"

"I didn't change my mind. . . . It was very hard for me to go back to the police. . . . I didn't want to talk about it."

"Well why did you suddenly change your mind about talking to them in January?"

"I had intended to earlier—but it was Christmas. . . ."

"But it took you three months to find a free day?"

"No, I—"

"It was three months, wasn't it?"

"Yes, but—"

"Did you talk to anyone about it before seeing Detective Jameson again?"

"Yes, yes, of course—"

"Who did you talk to?"

I knew what he was driving at; he was trying to imply the Rape Crisis Center drove me to do it. If I tried to cover the fact, I would get trapped. When in doubt, be honest and explain later.

"Someone from the Rape Crisis Center went with me to the police department that day."

He interrupted my answer with "No further questions."

I turned to Mr. Upchurch for a chance to explain what had been said between Carol and me, a chance to further explain that gap.

"No, your honor. I have no redirect."

"You may step down."

I was stunned. I looked at the judge then back to Upchurch. *Can't I . . . Wait there's more. . . . I can explain. . . . Upchurch?* . . . I was fully aware of what my last words were and their implication. Why had I given in to their game, I had been doing so well?

Rosemary and I went back upstairs to wait. I felt very exhausted and we talked quietly. I sat in the window sill that overlooked the town. The courthouse sat on a hill, making the world tiny and distant from where I sat. The gray stone wall of the old courthouse projected on the right side of the window. My mind was on the ancient blocks as Rosemary talked about how she was going to improve her compost pile. She knew I wasn't listening, and she hesitated occasionally. "Should I be quiet?" "No." She was nervous too. She went on to another topic that could occupy another three minutes. I was glad she was talking; it kept me in contact with reality as my mind wandered through "The Raven." I kept getting hung up on, "Quoth the raven, Nevermore." I wondered what was going on downstairs. I hoped Upchurch had cleared up any question about the time gap. At about five o'clock Jon came upstairs to tell me they were having closing arguments and I could go down to hear them.

When I walked into the courtroom, the judge was speaking. I realized he was finishing pronouncing the verdict, ". . . not guilty on counts one and two. Guilty on . . . Case dismissed."

"All rise. Court will resume session at ten o'clock tomorrow morning."

I didn't rise. I was straining to understand what I had heard.

"What was it, Karen?" She was beside me, but I didn't hear her answer either. She put her arms around me. The defendant rose and turned toward his lawyer. They shook hands and smiled. Something was very wrong. Jon had followed Mr. Upchurch out of the courtroom. Suddenly my rage exploded. I knew I had to get out of that room before I carried out my own justice. The trial was not supposed to end with the defendant smiling. I bolted out. It seemed as if thousands of people were in my way. I ran upstairs and sat down. Rosemary was right behind me. I looked up at her and started crying hysterically. She held me in her arms, cushioning my convulsive sobs. She was crying too. Finally the sobs quieted as I tried to regain control. *Think, Jenn, think. What happened? What was going on? It's what you*

*expected, isn't it? But everyone had said I was wrong. Ev-
eryone said it was a model case.*

Jon came in and tried to talk to me. I stared at the wall,
pounding reason into my mind. Karen came and put her
arms around me tightly. "Cry. Don't hold it back. Cry. It's
O.K." Why, Karen? Why cry? Why cry now? "What happened? I don't understand. What happened?" She suggested
I ask someone from the State's attorney's office, and she
went downstairs to get Ms. Parrish. Ms. Parrish came in and
sat down near me, waiting for me to speak.

"What happened?"

She told me the verdict, not guilty of rape or assault
with intent to commit rape, and told the judge's reasons.

"He said he had too many questions about that gap
with Jameson and about the role of the Rape Crisis Center.
But he believed you. He said you were an honest, sincere
witness. . . ."

"It was the gap, not whether or not it was rape. It was
just that stupid gap. Why didn't Upchurch let me explain?
It was Upchurch that blew it, not the judge!"

"Mr. Upchurch is a top-notch lawyer. I am sure he had
good reason for not pursuing it. That gap was not clear in
the police report. I wasn't aware of it, perhaps he wasn't either."

"I tried to tell him! If he had listened to me! Damn
him! There is no justice! What is the point of this farce! And
damn Upchurch can go home to his sweetie wife and laugh
about the absurd trial he had today. . . ."

"He's not like that, Jennifer. He is very upset. He didn't
expect to lose. He tried and he *is* a good lawyer."

"Then what happened? . . . Why? . . ."

I quieted down and a discussion ensued among those present about the justice system.

"It is the Miranda Act. . . ."

"It's the liberal concern for the 'poor prisoner' and prisoners' rights. . . ."

"The courts are overcrowded. . . ."

"The jails are overcrowded. . . ."

I listened but dismissed the reasons. There was something deeply wrong with a society that would allow this. Finally I let my thoughts out again. "But it's justice and truth that have lost value. There is no justice!"

"Yes, there is, Jennifer. Remember my ticket?" Karen was holding my hand to make me listen again to her story of the parking ticket she had gotten out of. It was a good story, but I wasn't listening this time. I looked at Karen and interrupted her.

"How do I explain this justice to Nigel? There is no justice. . . . Not when we were burglarized three times. Nothing but police forms to fill out, nothing more. . . . Not then and not now. . . . We had the guy this time! A million to one that he'd be caught, and this time they *had* him. . . . He's guilty. . . . It was going to be justice this time!" I screamed in frustration. My scream grew in intensity, and suddenly I realized I couldn't stop it. I screamed uncontrollably. The rage of all humankind stampeded out of my throat. I screamed until I had no voice to scream with and still my scream would not stop. I lost control of my body and my mind. I was drowning in my screams.

I don't know how long I screamed or how long I was quiet afterwards. Awareness returned when I realized I was not breathing. *Was this death? This strange stillness beyond emotions and sensations.* I thought of Nigel. I wanted to get back to him to explain. I opened my eyes and looked up at the bottom of the table. Realizing I wasn't dead and didn't want to die, I began gasping for breath. I looked up and saw Karen holding me and crying. I turned my head and saw Jon sitting helplessly under the table. He took my hand but there were no words. Finally I got the strength to sit up, but I was drained of any feeling. Ms. Parrish knelt beside me. I had forgotten she was there. She took my hand and arm with both her hands and said, "It may not mean a damn thing to you but I care, and if there is anything I can do to help, let me know." Tears softened her eyes, too.

"Can you tell me what to tell my three-year-old?"

She held my arm very tightly for a moment and then said, "He'll understand. He'll understand much more than most people ever do. He has a very brave, strong mother."

I smiled and a laugh and tears surfaced simultaneously at the absurdity. I looked up at Jon and he came to me immediately. I gripped him tightly and found reality returning to the room.

"What are we still doing in this silly room? I feel like I was born and died here." Or was it died and was born?

"What time is it anyway?" I could see it was dark outside and thought of our poor baby-sitter. Jon reassured me he had called her and everything was O.K. He had been out of the room calling her when I started screaming and had returned when my screams had died to gasps, finding me on the floor. *Poor Jon. Poor everyone who had had to endure this.* But I didn't feel embarrassed. It wasn't my fault. I couldn't prevent it.

"Don't be sorry, Jennifer. You've been building up to

that for a year. It's about time you got it out." *Oh, Karen, you always make me feel like I've done or said the best thing possible. I don't believe you but I love you for saying it.*

Many people called that night. I appreciated the calls and wanted to know who they were from, but I was too exhausted to talk. I wanted Jon to tell me everything that had happened that afternoon. After he had gone over the proceedings in detail enough times, I took one more Valium and went to sleep.

CHAPTER XII

IT WAS over except for the rage. I had been required to put all my trust in the system, I had turned over my mind for evidence, and they forgot I was a person.

JOURNAL - October 28, Thursday

Now that I have been thoroughly raped, I can fully understand people who want to take justice into their own hands. There has got to be a better system than one which allows the criminal to hire the best lawyer he can find and the victim to have a government bureaucrat put in his eight hours and let the victim hang. I do not pretend to understand the methods through which our legal system operates but I feel as if I was a pawn in a lawyer's game. Why would a lawyer even try to defend such a worm? That defense lawyer was actually trying to allow the pervert to walk away from it to strike again. Maybe next time it could be his wife and he might be concerned! It was all just an arena for the lawyers to display their technical skills, not a quest for justice. I could have survived better and given my testimony more clearly if Upchurch had stayed in bed yesterday! I might have been able to at least get the story out straight without all of his interruptions and I know I could have explained the gap and the Crisis Center. How could they not even know what the Crisis Center is? Why would the Crisis Center want to accuse a man they never met of rape when there are plenty of "honest rapists" to be had? Sending an innocent man to jail doesn't cut down on rapes. If I had wanted to change my story to rape, I certainly would have made up a better story, not sat there with such an obscure tale. When I knew the truth and had put all my energy into communicating that truth, it is devastating to hear that the judge had doubts. He had doubts about whether to believe I was honest and well-intentioned or whether I had been used by a "rape group" and lied about the rape aspect.

The defense argued that he wasn't the right man, it was misidentification. The defense never said it didn't happen the way I said it did until I was recalled to the stand. How can an argument say it's the wrong guy but even if it isn't the wrong guy, he didn't do it like she said he did? How could both pleas be made and the judge accept it? The judge didn't question the identification. How could he have said in his verdict that he thought I was sincere and honest yet believe I would concoct a rape line for the police three months later? I'm not sure my faith in our justice system can survive being betrayed by the very people who are appointed to protect the public. There is something absurd about the whole thing.

On Thursday I dealt with my emotions on the phone. I needed the reassurance that I was who I thought I was, someone to be believed and listened to. I needed to hear how well I'd done, to hear everyone else's rage, to be reassured it wasn't just my problem. I needed to hear all the details I could about what had actually happened on Wednesday, October 27.

After I talked to the people who had been there, I called Michelle. She had called on Wednesday night and Jon had asked her if she could take the kids for the weekend, I needed to talk to her about the arrangements. I had been aware that she hadn't called or asked about the trial, but I tried to ignore my hurt. I couldn't believe she wasn't concerned, still I wondered why she hadn't called. We talked for an hour and a half.

"I've been trying to call all week. When I couldn't even get Jon at the office, I knew it must be the trial. I'd be glad to take the kids. How are you doing?"

"It'll help so much if you took the kids for a few days till it calms down here. Jon could take them over on Saturday morning. I won't come though. I don't want to see Mom. Do you think you all could bring them back on Sunday? Just you, not with Mom?"

"Sure, Jenn . . . I . . . Can you tell me what happened?"

"It's a long story but I survived." And I gave her the details of the day, even the post-trial drama.

She was outraged by the outcome and cried during most of my story. "Jennifer, how can you take it! You're a pillar of strength!"

"Sure, Michelle. I had no choice. I tried to crack up, I even tried dying, but I didn't succeed at either, so I kept on living. There weren't any other choices."

"God, Jenn, I wish I could have been with you. I've been thinking about you day and night for the last week."

"I wish you had called. I would have liked for you to be with me."

"Jennifer! Your mom . . . Oh God." Her voice dropped. "I don't have to ask why you don't want to see your mom. I started to call you twice and she said not to bother you, you were doing fine, and you would call if you wanted to talk about it. We were sitting at the dining-room table last week and I said, 'I think I'll call Jenn,' and she sounded like she had talked to you recently and knew more than I did. Damn. I'm sorry. I should have called anyway. I wanted to. I'm sorry, Jenn." And her voice choked again.

"It's O.K., Michelle. I'm glad to hear you didn't forget me too."

For now I would ignore the rest of the family and hope that I would not need to face Mom. I couldn't face her "Hi, there. What's up?" smile as if nothing had been going on. Michelle was there and cared.

JOURNAL - October 31, Sunday

I realize now how unintimidated I am with men. Even attorneys, even judges on high benches are people too. I am so much more relaxed with everyone. Part of it is that the ultimate fear of men did happen. So much is knowing what I am capable of—the strength that surfaced when I had to have it, when I had no choice. Now I know where it is. Knowing what happens when I do lose control. It is the fear of the unknown that made me fear losing control so much. Now I know I can lose control and survive. I've spent so much time fighting my emotions in order to keep control but now I see that it isn't the end to lose control a bit. I have opened up in so many ways. I'm not afraid of showing emotion and I've learned the value of physical contact. Today after church, Pastor didn't say anything to me. He started to speak then just hugged me. It was a new experience to be able to accept open feelings in public. I am not sure this is me. I feel good and am in awe of myself as though I were a stranger.

Pastor called me later that day.

"I don't know what to say, Jennifer. You looked so pale and frail this morning."

"I'm O.K. I'm beginning to eat again. It was a rough week. I heard you were at the trial after lunch. I didn't know you were planning to be there."

"I didn't know if you wanted me there. I talked to Ava and she said she was going. It was a last-minute decision, but I was only there a couple hours. *I* was exhausted from it. I don't know how you did it. I got so angry . . . so angry. . . ."

"It wasn't very pleasant. Actually it was rather surrealistic." I didn't know what aspect of the trial he was reacting to.

"But he lied! They let him lie on the stand. . . ."

"I don't think it's meant to make sense."

"How do you feel about it now?" His voice softened as he turned to my feelings.

"Angry. Confused."

"Yeah. That makes sense. Would you like to get together to talk about it?"

"No, not yet. . . . I need to relax, forget it a bit. You're upset though, aren't you?" I felt guilty for refusing his request.

"Jennifer, I . . . it's . . ." His voice faltered. "It's been on my mind a lot."

"I'm O.K., Pastor. The worst is over. That's the important thing. It is finally over."

"Jennifer, you're an amazing woman."

"I had no choice. It's not amazing."

"Call me soon?"

"O.K."

We didn't talk about it again until much later, till I could talk about it quietly.

My math class was suffering from neglect, and I tried to pick it up again. After the deeply emotional exchanges I'd been a part of in the last week, it was hard to face the student banterings. The political combat was becoming heated as election time approached, and it seemed so superficial and trivial. The week after the trial, we returned from class break to find a fur coat had been stolen from the classroom. I was so upset I couldn't concentrate on the rest of class. Other people were shaken by the reality of a crime. As we walked out of class, two classmates walked with Rosemary and me, talking about the incident.

"Well, I'm sure whoever did it won't get away with it,

right there in the school. Someone would have seen it. And the police came so quickly," said the Girl Scout leader.

"Yes, our police force is really good, out here where we don't have much serious crime . . ." replied the gardener.

I couldn't hold back any longer. "It doesn't matter if he's caught anyway. There isn't any justice." They looked at me. "The system can't deal with a serious crime even. We weren't in class last week because we were at a trial. I was raped a year ago. There is no justice." It felt good to let it explode. Both Rosemary and I had been tempted to let them in on our private talks, but they seemed more concerned about centerpieces than people and we had refrained. Now it was out.

"Rape trials are supposed to be the worst kind. It's so good we have a Rape Crisis Center to deal with it." They escaped—handed it over to others. But the seed was planted before they turned off the path toward their car. Maybe they cried that night. Maybe they didn't think about it again. Maybe they thought I was strange, but it didn't matter. I felt good just letting it out. Someone was going to hear me sometime.

After that, emptiness set in. My spirits suffered from the nothing-left-to-talk-about syndrome. Time to forget it until I could find out when sentencing would be. They had set ninety days for presentencing investigation. That would put sentencing in January. Nothing more to think about or talk about. I began my retreat and wanted distance from those I had been so close to so recently. Within another week I began having nightmares again, not simple rape dreams but dreams of being badly abused and then laughed at by those I turned to for help. I suffered from flashbacks of the trial, as well as the assault. I was choking myself with anger.

JOURNAL - November 22, Monday

There are too many pressures. The kids need so much attention and patience. The less I give the more trouble they are and it adds to Jon's tensions and he's so depressed. Christmas is coming and there is no time. Wait! WAIT! Everything stop, freeze till I can sit down and think. Where is the final chapter to all this?

On December 2, I called to make an appointment to talk to Mr. Upchurch. I wanted to hear his side of the story. He was very friendly, saying, "I'm looking forward to seeing you again." His tone was very encouraging. Now I had to figure out what I was going to say to him.

In my anger I had rehearsed what I'd say to Upchurch if given a chance, but now I wanted him to understand my viewpoint, the viewpoint of a victim and a witness, and I wanted to hear his rationale of what happened. I wanted to blame him for what had happened but he was only a part of the system, the system that failed. I went to see him with questions, not accusations.

We talked for about two hours about a lot of aspects of the trial. He got off the subject often, as he had done before. He was especially wound up by a trial he had just finished, had just lost. I was sympathetic but kept pursuing my questions. He explained what the presentencing report was and what it was for. He explained about mistrials and appeals. It is customary for the defense to automatically file for an appeal, and he thought they probably had.

"The judge made a biased statement before the defense presented its case. They could try to use that to get a new trial. But he got off easy. What would they have to gain? The only thing he'd have to gain is the hope witnesses wouldn't appear at a later trial." He didn't think they would try for a new trial.

"If there was a new trial, what would that mean? When would it be?"

"It would be exactly like this trial, like this trial had never happened. It could take a year or more for a new trial. But don't worry about it, I don't think they would get it."

"Did you really expect a conviction on the rape charge?" I boldly leapt to the point of the meeting.

"Well, it was an iffy charge. The state always goes for the maximum charges possible. I don't think there was anything wrong with the charge though."

"So what went wrong?"

"I don't know. The judge obviously had doubts. I don't understand why it was a problem. It seemed perfectly acceptable to me. You didn't change your story. I didn't even think it needed explanation. And I don't see how who you talked to had anything to do with it. There was no reason for him to think you weren't being truthful. It was one of those cases like the case I just finished. Now there was an obvious case and the jury found him innocent. I can't understand it. How could they possibly? . . ."

"Yes, yes. It sounds like it was a bad verdict on that case. It must be hard for you not to talk about it, but I also wonder what happened to the 'assault with intent' charge?"

"Oh, that usually goes with the rape charge. When the rape was dismissed so was the intent charge."

"Wait a minute. So why have separate charges?"

"Well, like if a guy was caught in the act of rape, not quite rape, then he could be charged with intent."

"But didn't you say if he had thought that, for even a minute, it was intent?"

"Oh, but that is hard to prove."

"Did you try to prove it?"

"Look, I didn't think there was any problem with any of it. You told the story straight. The judge thought you were honest. I don't know what happened. I did my best and some things are beyond my control. I know that guy yesterday was guilty of armed robbery. I know it and I lost sleep all week over that and I lost. No, I didn't lose, I'm not supposed to look at it that way. But I do take it personally when I know I am prosecuting someone who is obviously guilty. Actually, in your case, I think the judge was too emotionally involved; he made some mistakes during the trial. This was his first rape case and he was expecting a jury trial. He was really affected by your testimony and may have bent over backwards to counteract it. I'm just guessing, but he was obviously very affected. That is a problem with new judges. But old ones have their problems too. They get too jaded. I had one case about three years ago where . . ."

"Yeah, well, it is getting late. How do you think the sentencing will go in my case considering he is a new judge?"

"He seems to be pretty strict from the little we've seen but. . . . I wish we could have emphasized the knife a bit more."

Yes, that was my other topic. "You didn't seem to pursue that at the trial."

"God, I tried every kind of question I could think of and it was like pulling hen's teeth to get you to mention it."

"Well, the defense kept objecting and confused me every time the knife was mentioned." *Was it me, not Upchurch, to blame for that? But he didn't ask the right questions or just let me tell it straight. If he had trusted me more to tell it, if we had talked more beforehand so I'd have known what was important. . . .*

"It was lucky we didn't have a sharp defense lawyer. He would have picked apart your identification statements. I was really surprised he didn't challenge that more. You never said the specifics that you observed, like the scar . . ."

"But I never saw the scar at the lineup. Don't you see, that was part of my description that I never observed again, but if it was there for others to see, it would have confirmed my identification. It could have been used in court to prove identification. I'm sure I told you I hadn't seen it. Did you see it? Did he have one?"

The discussion was beginning to raise more questions than it answered. I had wanted the court to assure me that it was the right guy, to decide whether or not it was rape, and both those questions were left for me to ponder on. It seemed if identification was an issue, they would have taken my police description and checked out the defendant themselves but they didn't. They didn't even have the composite picture to see if there was any resemblance. How could Upchurch blame me if the identification was weak? I was sure, and I did as well as I knew how to convey my certainty. Why didn't we go over that before the trial? My frustration was rising with my emotions.

"I just don't feel like anyone understands what it's like to be a victim. I didn't know anything about what was important to tell the police. I just answered their questions. It wasn't for me to judge what was important and what wasn't. I didn't know anything about trials and legal procedures, and everyone said just answer the questions the attorney asks. You are the professional, you're supposed to know what is important! I wanted to go over it all with you, but you didn't want to talk to me. I'd like to feel like a person again. Maybe now that the trial is over, after a year of this, maybe I can be human again. You have no idea what it's like to be a witness. I'd never been in a courtroom before. There's no way you'll ever know what it's like to be a rape victim. To be manipulated like a worthless object and then be manipulated by the courts on top of that. I'm sorry, I just can't stand the thought of what would have happened if this were a more complicated case." I couldn't hold back my frustrations any longer.

"I'm sorry, Mrs. Barr. I think I care even if no one could possibly understand. I've seen victims really messed up by this kind of crime. Victims that were afraid to go out of their houses alone, victims who couldn't possibly have even talked about the rape much less hold up under questioning. I may have seen more of the effects this kind of crime can cause than you have. . . ."

I couldn't stand it anymore. I was shaking and holding back the tears. *Is that what he thinks? That I shrugged my shoulders about the whole thing? That it wasn't really very upsetting to me? Could I possibly be such a good actress? Is this where all my efforts to be calm and rational have brought me?*

"I . . . I . . . It hasn't been easy. . . . It has been hell. . . . It's . . ." What could I say that would make him understand? Why should I expect him to understand? Why should I want him to understand? But I did.

His detachment had disappeared when I looked up at him as he spoke. "People need to have a philosophy of life . . . principles . . . like love. . . . Everyone needs to be loved by someone they respect. Your husband loves you. . . . He seemed concerned at the trial. My wife is wonderful. . . . I don't know what I'd do if anything ever happened to her. . . . If . . . I really need her. . . ."

I must have reached a sensitive chord in him someplace. I was almost frightened by the emotions he displayed. Somehow he found his way back to a more relevant subject. I guess we were both exhausted, and I had no more questions. He said he would let me know as soon as he found out when the sentencing would be.

I was drained but felt it had been a worthwhile meeting. I had asked all the questions I had on my list and expressed the frustrations I hadn't thought I could, and he had listened. I think he heard me.

In my attempts to get my thoughts under control, I had expelled the scapegoat for my anger. Upchurch had tried. I couldn't admit that I had anything to do with the lack of a total conviction at the trial, yet Upchurch had planted the seeds of doubt. If I couldn't blame Upchurch and if the judge erred because he was too sympathetic, who was left to blame but me? My anger turned inward. I was desperate for recognition and praise to use for ammunition against my

self-destructive thoughts. I wanted to forget the whole episode, yet I was obsessed by my anger. When the old fears
resurfaced, I grew angrier at myself. The harder I fought
the flashbacks the harder they attacked. I was blaming myself for everything that had gone wrong because I couldn't
find anyone else to blame and I had to put my anger someplace.

JOURNAL - December 13, Monday
Rosemary said the perfect thing after math class tonight.
She had been feeling guilty because she'd been jokingly
blaming me for being behind in math. I told her I was so
glad someone was feeling guilty about blaming me even
though she wasn't the one I needed to hear it from.

I avoided being with people because I was such a
grouch, and afterwards I was always critical of my behavior.
I was angry and impatient with everyone and most of all my
mother. With the trial over I tried to think how to deal with
her. I had to confront her with my feelings . . . that she had
deserted me. I was very bitter and I knew it would fester
until I told her. Each time I talked to her my feelings grew
as each time I saw her she offered no words of inquiry or acknowledgment about the trial. She planned a big family
gathering for Christmas and I told her simply, "I'd rather
not," and gave no further explanation.

When I saw my mother after Christmas, I decided it
was time to confront her. I had rehearsed my lines for more
than a month to make it as gentle as possible so that she
could understand. It would be my last effort to com-

municate with her on the topic. I desperately wanted it to be successful.

"Mom, I was hurt when no one called before the trial. I felt deserted." I had hoped the topic could have come up naturally, but it was 1 A.M. and time was running out on our visit. I couldn't put off talking about it any longer.

"Called? I thought you said you knew how to ask for help? If you had asked . . ."

"I'm not talking about asking for help. A call would have let me know you were thinking of me, that's all. You knew when it was. Just a call."

"Of course I was thinking of you. How could you think I could forget? But you said you could take care of yourself. I didn't want to call and remind you of it by asking. Sometimes it's better not to rub salt in the wounds as they say. But *you* wouldn't even talk about it. You didn't even tell me it happened for two weeks! You didn't even tell your own mother! How could I help when you wouldn't even tell me? . . . Everyone wanted to help and you rejected us all. You have been avoiding us . . . and when we see you, you are so serious and moody everyone is uncomfortable. If you wanted to talk about it, why didn't you call me? Jenn, I didn't even know it was rape till months later . . . till spring or later. I don't even know when . . . Oh, Jennifer, I've just wanted to hold you in my arms so many times. . . . If there was some way I could make it all better . . . but you haven't let anyone help. What could I do?"

She stopped talking and I looked up. Her face was red and tear-stained, but I wouldn't let her make me feel guilty about how I had reacted to my crisis.

"I'm not talking about a year ago. I'm talking about two

months ago. I was talking to anyone who'd listen and you
didn't. I stopped trying to talk to you when you changed the
subject every time it was mentioned." I had said too much. I
didn't want to argue.

"Mom, I just want you to know that I felt very deserted
when I didn't even get a call. I know it is hard for you to
talk about the rape. You would rather talk about pleasant
things. But I needed to know people cared more than I ever
needed anyone's support. . . ." I had said what I needed to
say. All I could say.

"Mom, maybe next time . . . maybe . . . It's O.K.,
Mom. I just had to say it. I couldn't pretend any longer."

"I never do anything right. How could I have let you
down so? I try. I really try. Why can't I ever do anything
right?" I hugged her, but I wouldn't soften what I had said.
I didn't know how it would affect her, but in expressing my
hurt, and hearing for the first time how she saw the situation, I could face her again without bitterness.

The confrontation with my mother removed a barrier
between us, but it did not ease the general depression that
was eating at me.

JOURNAL - January 5, Wednesday

Wish I knew what is bugging me. I really don't want to live
the rest of my life like this. How do I know I'm not crazy?
How long will the effects of all this last? Certainly other
people don't go through life with such depressions. I feel so
angry with nothing to focus my anger on—everyone is nice,
the trial is over, it went well, the guy will be punished. I'm
so tired of feeling angry. I don't want to see anyone because
I'll get perturbed and angry with them. I'm angry at myself

—always scolding myself. I hate it. Should I see Margot again or will I get sarcastic with her too? Where is the pill that'll make me "normal."

JOURNAL - January 11, Tuesday
"Victim Jennifer" gets so emotional and confused at times. I shut her in the closet for days then she jumps out on stage again. I wish I could get rid of her.

My dreams were still helpful in identifying my feelings. In January another dream helped identify my fears. I dreamed that at the sentencing it was proven that I was lying. I woke up screaming, trying to convince the world that it was all true. I decided to try Margot again.

"Jennifer, you have to stop thinking of yourself as a victim." *I know, Margot, that is why I'm here. I'm sick of it. I scream to make it go away. I want to be normal.*

"How do I do that?"

"You have to put it all behind you sometime."

"I'm not deliberately thinking about it. It just all comes back on me and it won't stop. I don't want to think about it. I don't want to be a victim anymore . . ." I was angry at the tears that interfered with my explanation.

"Jennifer, there's nothing anyone can do to make the flashbacks go away, but you don't have to dwell on them. You've come through so much. The sentencing will be this month, and that is the final step. It'll be over, and there is no sense allowing yourself to be a victim any longer. You've been through it all, and you've survived it all. It's over, Jennifer. It is up to you now to decide how long you're going to let it torment you. Do you see what you're doing to your-self?"

I saw. That's why I was there. *What good did it do for her to tell me to forget it, to get control of myself, when I yelled that to myself all day and it wouldn't work? Could she know the terror that still gripped me and still say to ignore the flashbacks and proceed as normal?* For the first time, I felt Margot couldn't understand. I didn't want to talk about it anymore. I couldn't suppress my thoughts, but I couldn't express them either. I couldn't push myself any longer. I wanted it to just go away.

She scheduled an appointment for the next week. I didn't fight it. I left the office more confused than ever. I wanted her to understand, to say, "I don't know what's going on in your mind but I want to understand." I wanted her to give me a solution. "Go swimming twice a day and your anger will go away." I wanted her to say, "It's normal." I wanted her to say, "Nothing is normal, things just happen inside minds. It will all go away when its time comes to be healed. If it was a physical wound, I'd give you a pain-killer until it healed, but it heals in its own time." Yes, that is what I wanted from Margot. She was my pain-killer until the wound healed, but it was the wrong potion this time. On the drive home, my mind filled in what I had missed from Margot that day.

My pain could run its course if I allowed it to. It was a scab that I kept picking at to make it go away, but the more I picked at it the more it bled. The pain existed. I could nei-ther deny it nor cure it. It had to heal in its own time. I had to stop interfering with the healing. My suffering lay in my fight to control my pain. The more I tried to control my thoughts and emotions, the angrier I got at my lack of control. I had to work on accepting the pain, but endurance required greater strength than conquest. Endurance was not a value nurtured by a society that believed in man's power to control the discomforts of life. I had to learn how to endure and I had to do it alone.

Finally, in learning to accept pain, even death, a calmness filled me and encircled me. My expectations of life became more realistic. My values became clear and I could stop listening to the values of others. I stopped believing in the Pepsi Generation.

I canceled my appointment with Margot on the same day I learned that the sentencing was scheduled for the next week. I didn't want to talk to Margot about it. I wasn't ready to defend the thoughts that made me feel comfortable.

I went to the sentencing to witness the final step. Friends who I talked to about it all seemed to hope for a stiff sentence. I didn't put my hopes in years, I just hoped that somehow the system could prevent this man from doing further harm.

Kathy called unexpectedly and asked why I even wanted to go to the sentencing.

"Haven't you been through enough?"

"I just want to see the end. This time I can sit back and just watch."

"Do you need a baby-sitter that day? I could watch the kids for you."

"Kathy, how good of you. As a matter of fact, I do need a sitter. Thanks so much." I was grateful for the offer but more excited to hear Kathy finally acknowledge the reality of my situation.

Rosemary and I entered the courtroom after the judge had begun speaking. Each of the lawyers was to make a statement of his opinion on the sentence. Mr. Upchurch asked for the maximum sentence and gave his reasons. The defense made a request for a new trial and it was granted.

I felt Rosemary tense as she turned to me to confirm what she had heard. I didn't return her glance. I knew what I had heard. It was because of the judge's premature verdict. I stared at the back of the defendant's head. It was somehow comical. The defense attorney stood and stared absently at me, and I felt that if I returned his stare I would start to giggle at the absurdity of it all. For a moment it seemed that the defendant and I were both caught in the lawyers' games. But he didn't know he was a pawn too. He thought he had drawn a winning card. I felt sorry for his thinking that he could gain something by this maneuver, but he had a right to his hopes no matter what it cost him. I knew I had no choice but to return, and this time I would know the game.

That night my mother called.

"Hi, Jenn. Just thought I'd call to see what's happening. How're the kids? What have you been up to lately?"

For a moment I thought she knew.

"Oh, it's so nice of you to call, Mom. I . . ." and my tenseness came laughing out. "Sorry, Mom. It's nothing. I was just thinking about a funny thing Nigel said the other day. He's such a nut. . . ."

THE LAST CHAPTER

In April I learned that the new trial was scheduled for July 5. Once I knew the date, I could not push it out of my mind any longer. I began another descent into depression, though anger had replaced fear of the unknown, and disillusionment had replaced idealism. "Why should I go through with this again? Why should I join in their circus? Hadn't I given enough of myself already?" I needed to believe my blood was going to a worthy cause. My desire to make life rational was again dragging me down until the laughter broke loose and I let go. I knew their game this time and I would play the game according to their rules. The goal wasn't justice, it was winning, and the rule was every man for himself. When I walked into the courtroom the second time, I was a player not a pawn. A young lawyer had been assigned by the State's attorney's office. ("We like to rotate the attorneys to keep them from getting stale.") When we met, I asserted my game plan to him. "I do not want my address publicly announced in the courtroom, and I would like to be able to tell what happened without interruptions, without having to give it out piecemeal in answer to your questions." The new lawyer had never prosecuted a felony case before and accepted my suggestions.

On the morning of the second trial, the defense attorney offered to plea-bargain. I was consulted about the offer of a guilty plea by the defense if the State would ask for only a five-year sentence. Though the lawyers were not bound by my opinion, I felt less powerless to be a part of the decision. I was ready to proceed with the trial, and the plea-bargain offer served to strengthen my confidence. The defense would not have made the offer at that point unless he was worried. I was willing to take the risk and we proceeded with the trial.

Re-telling the details of the rape was no easier than the first time, but I was more prepared to defend my story during the cross-examination. It seemed that the defense attorney had hoped for a worn-down witness at this second trial, twenty-one months after the case began. Instead he found a stronger, more confident witness. He misquoted statements I had made in the first trial, not realizing that the first trial was as etched in my mind as the rape itself. When I left the stand, I had no feelings of triumph or of frustration. I had finished what I had to do and would wait to learn the final results of my efforts. I had spun the wheel but did not cross my fingers for a winning number. The number the wheel would land on was no longer a concern of mine.

I waited in the courthouse again as I had been instructed and was notified in time to hear both the closing arguments and the verdict. The defense attorney used the same distortions in his closing statement that he had tried to use during my testimony. I wondered how well the judge would remember my statements. Before the judge gave his verdict, he reviewed the case as he saw it. "For the participants in a trial, there is an advantage in having a trial by judge rather than by jury. A jury cannot give the reasons for its verdict but that restriction does not hold for a judge." He proceeded to weigh every piece of evidence and every conflicting issue. "In the question of identification, I compared the defendant very carefully with the description Mrs. Barr gave to the police, the *detailed* description she gave. I observed every detail down to the position of the scar on the defendant here today." Finally someone had taken the effort to confirm my identification! In his verdict the judge said to the defendant, "We are all lucky today. If Mrs. Barr had not been able to stay calm during the ordeal, I believe that this could have been a murder trial." I was finally assured that someone appreciated the gravity of the case.

Since the defendant had been found not guilty of rape and assault with intent to commit rape at the first trial, he could not be retried on those charges. But he was again found guilty of all the remaining counts—perverted sex acts, assault, and battery. The man who had nearly destroyed me was sentenced to ten years in jail plus five years' probation. I did not have enough idealism left to hope that he could be reformed in ten years, but it was a few years less that he would be a threat to anyone.

I left the courtroom with a feeling of freedom I hadn't known for twenty-one months. My only concerns were for the victims not as lucky as I was.